LECTURES DELIVERED UNDER
THE AUSPICES OF THE WALKER-AMES FOUNDATION
AT THE UNIVERSITY OF WASHINGTON
APRIL, 1942

RELIGION AND EMPIRE

Religion and Empire

The Alliance
between Piety and Commerce
in English Expansion
1558–1625

By

LOUIS B. WRIGHT

OCTAGON BOOKS

A DIVISION OF FARRAR, STRAUS AND GIROUX

New York   1973

Reprinted 1965
by special arrangement with The University of North Carolina Press

Second Octagon printing 1973

OCTAGON BOOKS
A DIVISION OF FARRAR, STRAUS & GIROUX, INC.
19 Union Square West
New York, N. Y. 10003

LIBRARY OF CONGRESS CATALOG CARD NUMBER: 65-25894
ISBN 0-374-98816-1

Printed in U.S.A. by
NOBLE OFFSET PRINTERS, INC.
NEW YORK, N.Y. 10003

Preface

A CONGENIAL alliance between religion and trade in the late sixteenth and early seventeenth centuries profoundly influenced the beginnings of what would one day become the British Empire. It has been my purpose here to describe briefly the partnership between the English clergy and the commercial companies which developed trade with the East and began the colonization of North America. The propaganda and influence of the clergy were powerful factors in creating public sentiment for expansion overseas.

Although sixteenth- and seventeenth-century Englishmen generally did not think of overseas colonies in terms of later eighteenth-century imperialism, a few political thinkers were aware of the political implications of colonial expansion. The clergy gave expression to some of the more advanced ideas of imperialism in this period. Much of their reasoning concerning empire was based on the examples of the empires of Rome and Spain. It is not my contention, however, that the clergy prior to 1625 anticipated the imperialism of the late eighteenth century. I merely want to indicate the nature of their thinking about territorial expansion and to emphasize their influence in shaping English ideas in that direction.

The story of the religious motives which led to the settlement of New England has been often told and frequently exaggerated. But the influence of the clergy as agents of propaganda for expansion in the preceding period has been very nearly overlooked. Alexander Brown, in *The Genesis of the United States*, it is true, printed excerpts from most of the pertinent sermons on Virginia, but the significance of these sermons has escaped notice. The fact is that late Elizabethan and Jacobean preachers, Anglicans and Puritans alike, were keenly aware of the necessity of checkmating Spain, and they waged an incessant campaign to arouse the English nation to awareness of the danger that threatened it. Spain, to discerning Englishmen of the period, occupied much the same position as Nazi Germany does today. England as a whole, however, was only dimly conscious of the implications of the Spanish empire, and many Englishmen were ardent isolationists, asleep alike to the rich opportunities of expansion and the hazards of allowing Spain to seize all of the New World. The Protestant clergy, with their traditional hatred of Catholic Spain, set to work to shake England out of its lethargy. They succeeded in paving the way for empire.

The part that the Puritan clergy played in developing New England falls outside the scope of the present study. I have confined my discussion principally to a consideration of the preparatory and experimental period that coincided with the late years of Elizabeth and the reign of James I. In those years, the public came to realize that England had a great destiny overseas. In creating this opinion, the clergy had a tremendous influence.

The seven chapters printed here were delivered as lectures on the Walker-Ames Foundation at the University of Washington in April, 1942. The original lecture form has been necessarily retained. Hence there is a certain amount of repetition of ideas, unavoidable in lectures designed for delivery to a public audience not always the same.

To President L. P. Sieg and the Regents of the University I am under especial obligations. They have made possible the appearance of these lectures in their present format. I wish to thank particularly Dean Frederick M. Padelford, Professor Dudley D. Griffith, the members of the English and history departments, and many other members of the faculty for the cordial and gracious hospitality extended to me as one of the visiting lecturers on the Walker-Ames Foundation.

I am especially indebted to my friend, the late Professor Ray Heffner, for many stimulating discussions concerning the theme of these lectures. His death was a tragic loss, not only to the University of Washington, but also to American scholarship.

For advice about many points in this little book, I am grateful to my colleagues Professors Edwin Gay and Godfrey Davies, and to Professors Robert G. Cleland, Fulmer Mood, William Huse Dunham, and David H. Willson. Mr. Merrill H. Crissey, of the editorial staff at the Huntington Library, and Miss Sadie Hales and Mrs. Marion Tinling have been exceedingly helpful in preparing the manuscript for the printers and in making the index.

L. B. W.

The Huntington Library

San Marino, California

May 20, 1942

Contents

RELIGION AND EMPIRE

CHAPTER ONE

Elizabethan Adventurers
and the Providence of God

LANDSMEN who cluster in cities and contrive ingenious machines to do their bidding find it easy to magnify their own importance, to forget their ancient fears of the gods, and to laugh at the superstitions of simpler folk. But the men who pit their strength against elemental nature, especially those who follow the sea, have never been complacent of their own powers. They who have experienced the sudden violence of Neptune, or God, or Satan, or maybe, in a later day, merely "the old devil, the sea," know that there is a strength beyond the strength of men, something all-powerful and supernatural. And, while landsmen have sometimes scoffed, seamen, wicked though they may be, have kept a healthy respect for a divinity that shapes their courses and sends hurricanes, waterspouts, or fair winds.

Few seamen more daring than Queen Elizabeth's freelance adventurers have ever sailed the seas. They pushed their frail craft into the teeth of tropical storms and skirted

the grinding ice packs of the Arctic. They harried the great
ships of Spain, fought many times their numbers, and
robbed and burned the fabulous cities of New Spain. During momentary lulls in their warfare, they risked capture
and traded with their traditional enemy, supplying slaves
hazardously taken on the pestilent shores of Guinea. In
strange regions they landed and explored territory never
before visited by white men. They suffered hunger and
thirst, heat and cold, scurvy and plague, but in the end
they established England as a sea power—indeed, as the
first sea power of the world. They were afraid of no man.
Irreverently, they flouted the King of Spain and the Pope
of Rome. They stood in awe and in fear of only two
powers, the Queen of England and the Protestant Jehovah.

Of the two it is hard to say who caused sixteenth-century
buccaneers more concern, God or the Queen. In any case,
they took care to placate both. They sacrificed a goodly
portion of their booty to the earthly deity in Whitehall,
and they supplicated the celestial authority with prayers
and thank offerings. In many instances, they carried chaplains in their ships to give a color of piety to their undertakings and to implore heaven to bless them.

Modern editors of the narratives of sixteenth- and seventeenth-century voyages have sometimes wondered whether
the pious professions of shipowners and ship captains were
sincere or were merely "a concession to a prevailing cant." [1]
That they represented a genuine faith in the providence of
God cannot be doubted by anyone who has studied the
religious background of Elizabethan England. It does not

necessarily follow that these seafarers were themselves pious men, given to prayer and psalm singing; but few, even among the most iniquitous of them, would have had the temerity to express a doubt of divine intercession, and most had a positive faith that God kept an ever-watchful eye and would curse them for wickedness and blasphemy as he might bless them for obedience, adoration, and praise. This positive faith, this simple belief that God watched over and protected the faithful as he likewise punished the errant, was the common belief of all England, Catholic, Anglican, and Puritan alike. Theirs was still an age of faith, and the frequent references to the providence of God, though sometimes conventional in expression, nevertheless are evidences of beliefs that were genuine and unshakable. Pious observations, set down in ships' logs, strike the modern reader as strangely out of place, for we no longer think of seafarers as godly men. But in the sixteenth and early seventeenth centuries these comments were expressive of the temper of the times. Similar observations can be found in vast abundance even in the business correspondence of the day.

Religion was a motive of greater consequence in early British expansion than we have hitherto realized. Although we have overemphasized the desire for freedom of worship as a motive in the settlement of New England, we have forgotten or discounted the religious fervor which inspired some of the propaganda for earlier exploration and colonization. The need for converting the heathen to Protestant Christianity was a recurring theme in English discussions of colonization. The stress upon this high purpose did not diminish in the least the promise of rich material profits to be derived from foreign enterprise. Indeed, Tudor and Stuart Englishmen profoundly believed that a partnership with God was likely to provide a safe insurance against disaster and loss. Furthermore, a missionary purpose helped to enlist the favor of the preachers, the most active and articulate propagandists of the age, who forthwith became diligent spokesmen for all kinds of overseas ventures. Because the English public awoke slowly to the possibilities of colonial expansion, the blessings of the clergy proved useful in stirring up potential investors in voyages of discovery and settlement. To say, as one historian has remarked, that the idea of converting the heathen appealed to "but a limited number of minds," and hence "no great stress need be laid upon it,"[2] is to disregard the tremendous influence that Christian motives exerted, directly and indirectly, upon even the most materialistic adventurers of that day.

The attitude toward religion of the great commanders of Elizabethan voyages ranged from unadulterated self-interest to high idealism. Some took along a chaplain merely for protection—a sort of living talisman against bad luck. A few were sincerely concerned about the spiritual welfare of their men and the godless plight of heathen whom they might encounter. But most of those who expressed themselves on religious questions indicate a mingling of motives: religion was good for discipline on board ship; prayers and piety brought upon a voyage the favor of the Almighty; and the conversion of the heathen tended to the glory of God and the benefit of the English nation.

In various forms, sometimes briefly, sometimes in lengthy disquisitions, Elizabethan adventurers set forth these views.

Among the seamen, piety, religious observances, and a desire to convert the heathen were not restricted to puritanical sectarians; nor, indeed, were they a monopoly of English voyagers. From the very beginning of the voyages of western discovery, religion had occupied a prominent place in the asserted motives of explorers. For example, mingled with the hope of private profit, which Columbus had held out to his backers, was the promise of winning new realms for Christendom and bringing about the conversion of thousands of lost souls "to the holy faith of Christ." [3] Through his writings runs this constant theme. Priests accompanied the sailors and soldiers of Spain, and the missionary zeal of the Spanish was second only to the greed for gold and land as a motivation of their colonial enterprises. They also commanded religious observances in their fleets. When Medina Sidonia was preparing to launch the great Armada attack on England in 1588, he issued general orders to all ship commanders to see that their crews were shriven and received the Sacrament with "contrition for their sinnes." [4] And to prevent further sinfulness, he gave detailed orders which, in their severity, would have shamed an English Puritan. Particularly, commanders were instructed to see that no sailor or soldier should "blaspheme, or rage against God, or our Lady, or any of the Saints," even in the stress of battle.

From the start of English exploration, religious observances conducted by the ship's chaplain were a part of the daily routine in many voyages. One of the earliest recorded English ship chaplains was an adventurous canon of St. Paul's, who sailed with an expedition of two ships sent out by Henry VIII on May 20, 1527, to explore the coast of Labrador. His name has been forgotten, but he was "a great Mathematician," "indued with wealth," and he helped to fit out the ships, one of which was piously christened "Dominus Vobiscum," "a name likely to be given by a religious man of those dayes," Richard Hakluyt remarks.[5] For the expedition in search of a Northeast Passage to Cathay, led by Sir Hugh Willoughby and Richard Chancellor in 1553, old Sebastian Cabot drew up a set of ordinances which prescribed "morning and evening prayer, with other common services appointed by the kings Majestie, and other lawes of this Realme to be read and saide in every ship daily by the minister in the Admirall, and the marchant or some other person learned in other ships, and the Bible or paraphrases to be read devoutly and Christianly to Gods honour, and for his grace to be obtained, and had by humble and heartie praier of the Navigants accordingly." [6] Richard Stafford was the minister appointed to go with Sir Hugh in the "Bona Esperanza"; [7] yet, despite the good name of their vessel and the daily supplication of grace, they were cast away and perished miserably on the Russian coast, near Murmansk, in the winter of 1554. But Cabot's pious instructions became a part of the rules governing countless voyages for more than a century.

No voyage was too dubious and no sailors too conscienceless to seek the benefits of divine blessing on their enterprises. The various voyages led by members of the Hawkins family, for instance, were not precisely Sunday School picnics, and the Hawkinses, by strict standards, were far from being exemplary Christians; but they sometimes sounded like clerics and made rules that would have been a credit to the vicar of a peaceful parish. When Sir John Hawkins, in command of the flagship "Jesus of Lubeck," led a slaving expedition to Guinea and thence to the Spanish West Indies in 1564–65, he summarized his special orders for the voyage with these practical and pious injunctions: "Serue God dayly, loue one another, preserve your victuals, beware of fire, and keepe good companie." [8] The names of the ships often smacked of religion. With unconscious irony, the chronicler of the voyage tells of the sailors' joy when the "Jesus" overtook the "John the Baptist" of London and added it to the expedition. Later, when the ships, crowded with negro slaves, were becalmed off Sierra Leone and the water supply almost gave out, Hawkins' faith in Providence was justified, for "Almightie God, who neuer suffereth his elect to perish," sent a northwest wind that carried the fleet quickly to Santo Domingo. [9] Like Peter Faneuil, a Boston slave trader of a later day, Hawkins believed that he had performed a Christian service in bringing benighted heathen to a land where they might be baptized and receive the blessings of salvation. Religious language came easily to Hawkins' lips. With some unction, he excused his failure to intercept the Spanish treasure fleet in 1590 by reminding Queen Elizabeth that "Paul planteth and Apollos watereth, but God giveth the increase"—which is said to have provoked the Queen to exclaim, "This fool went out a soldier, and is come home a divine."[10] Soldier, buccaneer, or divine, Sir John understood and used on occasion the idiom of the church; a poem attributed to him, in praise of Sir Humphrey Gilbert's expedition to North America in 1583, asserts that zeal for religion, the country's welfare, and material profit all combine to urge support of colonization:

Whence glory to the name of God, & countries good shall spring,
And vnto all that further it, a priuate gaine shall bring. . . .

The yssue of your good intent, vndoubted will appeare,
Both gratious in the sight of God, and full of honour heere.[11]

Richard Hawkins, the son of Sir John, inherited not only his father's skill in seamanship but something also of his belief in the practical value of piety. His rambling treatise entitled *Observations . . . In His Voiage Into The South Sea. Anno Domini 1593* [12] attributes to God his escapes from danger. The reason the Spaniards have been especially blessed in their overseas endeavors, Hawkins points out, may be found in the Almighty's desire to reward them for their noteworthy obedience to His commands. To secure the divine blessing upon his own enterprise, Hawkins provided that the Sabbath should be "reserved for God alone." But there were limits to his godliness. For instance, he objected without avail when his mother-in-law christened his ship the "Repentance." Though the good woman asserted that "repentance was the safest ship we could sayle in to purchase the haven of Heaven," Hawkins thought it an "uncouth name" and was pleased when the Queen also "disliked" it and rechristened the vessel the "Daintie."

From the first voyage of Martin Frobisher, in 1576, onward, the conversion of the heathen became an increasingly prominent motive in the discussions of westward expansion. Merchants, seamen, and preachers all joined in emphasizing the worthiness of missionary endeavors. Preachers eagerly joined the exploring expeditions, but they showed little desire to remain among the Indians and Eskimos. Instead, they returned to describe the wonders of the New World and to add their voices to the growing chorus urging colonial settlement.

No clergyman, however, could sound more like a missionary than Captain George Best, who went with Frobisher on his voyages in search of the Northwest Passage and wrote an account of their adventures. "By our Englishmen's industries, and these late voyages," he observes in the dedication of his work to Sir Christopher Hatton, "the world is grown to a more fulnesse and perfection; many unknowen lands and ilands (not so much as thought upon before) made knowen unto us; Christ's name spred; the Gospell preached; infidels like to be converted to Christianitie, in places where before the name of God had not once bin hearde of." [13] Every event of the voyages, in Captain Best's opinion, was the result of God's direct intervention. On the first voyage, one of Frobisher's men had picked up a piece of ore believed to contain gold. Later, when diligent search failed to reveal any further traces of gold, Best sanctimoniously concluded that the original discovery was a miracle in that God had directed an Englishman to the only rich stone on the island because His "divine will and pleasure is to have oure common wealth encreased with no lesse abundance of His hyden treasures and golde mynes than any other nation." As an afterthought he added the wish that "the fayth of His Gospell and holy name should be published and enlarged throughe all those corners of the earth, amongst these idolatrous infidels." [14]

On Frobisher's third voyage to the Northwest, in 1578, Lord Burleigh himself gave special instructions that there should be a minister to conduct divine services "accordying to ye churche of England," [15] and the Privy Council wrote to the Bishop of Bath asking that a certain parson named Wolfall be encouraged to go with the expedition "in respect of the necessitie that such a companie should be exercised in Religion." [16] Frobisher received written instructions to banish from the fleet swearing, dice and card-playing, and filthy communication, and to "serve God twice a day, with the ordinarie service, usuall in churches of England." [17] In times of danger and after miraculous escapes, special prayers were said in the ships, with the whole company gathered about the mainmast. [18] Even the watchword sounded like a biblical paraphrase from a sermon. The fleet received orders that any vessel approaching in the night should be hailed with the words, "Before the world was God," and, if the challenged vessel belonged to their company, the watch was to reply, "After God came Christ, his Sonne." [19]

Master Wolfall, the chaplain, proved himself worthy of his trust and won high praise from the chronicler of the voyage. He was no youth, fresh from the university and eager for excitement, but a settled minister of reputation, who left a comfortable living and a devoted wife and children in order to bring the voyage to perfection, to save souls, and to reform infidels to Christianity. He diligently preached to the mariners, visiting the ships by turn, and would have remained a year among the Eskimos "if occasion had served, being in every necessary action as forward as the resolutest men of all." [20]

Though simple piety and a zeal for Christianity inspired chaplains like Master Wolfall, these things alone do not account for the interest in religion displayed by some of the seagoing adventurers. Matters of state and religion were inextricably mixed in the politics that determined the nature of many important voyages. Protestant Englishmen had long hated and feared Catholic Spain, but until the last quarter of the sixteenth century they did little to keep Spain from carving out a new Catholic empire in America. In the 1570's, however, the so-called Puritan party, headed by the Earl of Leicester and ably guided by Sir Francis Walsingham, awoke to the danger and set about checking Spain's imperialistic ambitions. This group, which became the party of English expansion, soon found itself opposed by a strong conservative faction whose leader was no less a person than Burleigh, the Lord Treasurer; he hoped to keep the peace and circumvent Spain by diplomacy. But the slow and devious methods of diplomatic maneuver did not appeal to men like Drake, Gilbert, and Raleigh. Believing that more direct action was required, they fought Spain on the high seas and tried to establish a foothold for Protestants on the American mainland. In letters, treatises, and public utterances, the expansionists emphasized religion—Protestant religion—as a motive. Much of the talk of carrying salvation to the heathen, of saving the New World from popery, was doubtless sincere. Certainly it was an excellent item of propaganda in a country emotionally aroused against Spain and the Catholics.

In the voyages of Sir Francis Drake, most famous of Queen Elizabeth's seamen and inveterate enemy of Spain, not much was said about the conversion of the infidels but there was more than a little talk of religion. Among the buccaneers who preyed on Spanish shipping, Drake was the best hater of papists. In his opinion, an attack on Spain was a blow for the true faith and a stroke against anti-Christ. Drake's voyages therefore became crusades against the powers of darkness, and he became the hero of countless English parsons who forgot the pirate in the glorification of Christ's emissary.

From boyhood Drake himself had experienced the combined influences of Protestant religion and the sea. His father appears to have been a sort of lay preacher, a type common among the later Puritans; during the reign of Edward VI, he procured a post as reader of prayers to seamen in the King's navy and had for his dwelling the floating hulk of a ship. Like other west-country Protestants, Drake's father was bitterly hostile to Catholics and he must have imbued his sons with his own faith—as well as a hatred of the great Catholic sea power which the sailors who came into Plymouth harbor described in many a tale of horror. In his will, the father commended the beginning of the Book of Romans and urged his sons to make much of the Bible.[21] What fanatical purpose and inner strength Francis Drake's religious background gave him, we can only guess, but it was no inconsequential factor in making him a successful foe of Spain.

When Drake set sail from Plymouth on November 15, 1577, on the voyage that was to take him around the world, he carried for the instruction of his men Bibles, prayer books, and Foxe's *Book of Martyrs,* and had, for chaplain, one Francis Fletcher, a parson whose energy in preaching and praying sometimes outran his discretion. Routine religious duties were as rigorously enforced as any other discipline of the ship, and in times of crisis the commander prescribed special religious exercises. When Thomas Doughty was court-martialed for seditious conspiracy and sentenced to death, Drake devoutly took communion with his prisoner before he ordered him beheaded.[22] A little later Drake went ashore with all his men and ordered them to confess their sins and take communion. The chaplain offered to preach a sermon but the commander stopped him. "Nay, soft, Master Fletcher," he cautioned, "I must preach this day myself." [23] The "sermon" that followed was a rousing speech on loyalty and obedience, with a challenge to the courage of Englishmen to see their task well accomplished.

Sermons were frequent on this voyage and no event of importance passed without official commentary from the chaplain. When Drake changed the name of his ship from the "Pelican" to the "Golden Hind," Master Fletcher brought the ceremonies to a conclusion with a sermon "teaching true obedience," followed by prayers "and giuing of thankes for her maiesty and most honorable counsell, with the whole body of the common weale and church of God." [24] After passing Cape Horn Drake intended to land and leave a monument to Queen Elizabeth and have a sermon to solemnize the event, but the weather proved too bad for so patriotic and godly a gesture.[25] The commander was not far behind his preacher in ability to exhort and quote Scripture. To encourage his half-frozen men in the icy seas off the northwest coast of America, he made them "comfortable speeches of the diuine prouidence," and cited biblical examples of "God's louing care ouer his children." [26] So stirred were the sailors by these and other "profitable persuasions" that they acquitted themselves with fortitude and ceased to grumble. After making a landing on the coast of California, Drake and his men, in the presence of the Indians, fell to their knees in prayer; and then, by pointing upward, they tried in pantomime to teach these heathen that the true God whom they ought to worship was in heaven above. The Indians, the chaplain reported in his journal, listened attentively to the prayers and the reading of the Scriptures, and particularly rejoiced at the singing of Psalms. So great was their pleasure in this exercise that they frequently resorted to the shore and by intoning a phrase signified that they wanted more Psalm singing from the sailors.[27] Thus was the first gospel message brought by Protestants to the heathen of California.

Drake's piety was so deeply engrained that, in the face of imminent disaster, he took time to implore divine help. His narrowest escape came in January, 1579, when the "Golden Hind" ran aground on a shoal in the South Pacific. As the ship seemed about to split, he gave orders for prayers and made some "comfortable speeches of the ioyes of that other life," not neglecting, however, to man the pumps and to set an example of diligence to the crew. To strengthen their faith, Drake ordered the chaplain to administer the Sacrament and to preach a sermon. Then they lightened the ship and miraculously floated free.[28]

In the stress of danger, the chaplain had touched on things better left unsaid, even in addressing God, and Drake's wrath now consumed him. The precise nature of the offense is obscure. Previously Drake had treated the chaplain well. At the sack of Santiago, for example, he personally gave him the loot from the chapel, consisting of a silver chalice, two cruets, and an altar cloth—fit trophies for a Puritan preacher.[29] But Fletcher had been one of Doughty's defenders, and, after the execution, had, on occasion, hinted that God might send a judgment upon the expedition. In his last sermon, while the ship was aground, the minister had apparently played on that theme once too often. Probably interpreting the sermon as a rebuke for the execution of Doughty, Drake put the preacher in irons and called the ship's company together. As if burlesquing a bishop, Drake sat in judgment, cross-legged on a chest, waving a shoe in his hand. He declared the chaplain excommunicated out of the Church of England and denounced him to the "divell and all his angells." He forbade him, on pain of being hanged, to appear before the mast again and ordered him to wear about his neck a posy bearing the legend, "Francis Fletcher, ye falsest knave that liveth." [30] So ended the ministry of Drake's energetic chaplain, and at this point also ended his journal with its edifying reports on the piety of the commander and the religious exercises on the first English voyage around the world. As a friend of Doughty's, Fletcher had small love for Drake, but, as a preacher, he could not help taking a professional pride in the great seaman's religious discipline. Fletcher's description of the religious exercises during the voyage is confirmed in other documents.

Drake fared well at the hands of the preachers, who trumpeted his fame long after his death. Their praise was well merited, for he devoted his life to warring against the arch-enemy of all Protestant powers, and in their eyes was an appointed instrument of God's vengeance. True, he had often robbed and pillaged peaceful towns and ships, but in a conflict with the Amalekites a leader of Israel could do no wrong. Drake's apotheosis as a national hero owed much to the clergy, who were ever ready to glorify a seaman if he smote the Spanish papists hip and thigh. If he also had breath for a prayer and a word of Scripture, he was only little lower than the angels. In the next generation, Philip Nichols, chaplain of the expedition against the Spanish coast in 1587, wrote an account of Drake's voyage to the West Indies in 1572–73 and the capture of Nombre de Dios. The very title, *Sir Francis Drake Reuiued: Calling vpon this Dull or Effeminate Age, to folowe his Noble*

18

Steps for Golde & Siluer . . . (1626), was intended to magnify the deeds of the godly buccaneer and rebuke sluggards of a more peaceful day. Nichols' book was an authorized narrative, which had the editorial supervision of Drake's namesake and heir, Sir Francis Drake, Baronet. Two years later came another authorized account, supervised by the nephew and based on a preacher's journal—a fact that the title-page was careful to emphasize. The second work, already quoted here, was called *The World Encompassed . . . Carefully collected out of the Notes of Master Francis Fletcher, Preacher in this imployment, and diuers others his followers in the same* . . . (1628). Though Drake had characterized Fletcher as the greatest rogue that ever lived, ironically he owed much of his reputation in later generations to the chaplain's narrative.

Chaplains in some of the voyages exerted an influence in excess of their normal duties as pastors of their seagoing flocks. The most conspicuous example of the power of seafaring preachers occurred in an expedition which set out from Southampton in May, 1582, under the leadership of Captain Edward Fenton. Its main object was trade. The Privy Council instructed Fenton to go to the East Indies and Cathay by way of the Cape of Good Hope and on the return to seek the Northwest Passage from the Pacific side. These instructions specified that he was to have an executive committee composed of eight men besides himself, who would determine all "waightie causes." Two of the eight were ministers: the Reverend Richard Madox, fellow of All Souls College in Oxford, and the Reverend John

Walker. Both preachers were of the Puritan group and both were protégés of the Earl of Leicester, who had a great interest in the voyage.[31]

The Privy Council's instructions were more than usually specific, particularly concerning the responsibilities and privileges of the preachers. Madox, the senior chaplain, was to serve as secretary and keep for the Council a secret record of every happening. Walker likewise, in another ship, was to keep a careful record. Madox also carried one of the three keys to the two caskets containing wax balls in which had been sealed Her Majesty's orders concerning the command in case of Fenton's death. At all deliberations of the ships' officers Madox had to be present. The two ministers were advised to take up their quarters by turns in each of the four ships. Finally, Fenton's instructions read, "to the end God may blesse this voyage with happie and prosperous successe, you shall have an especiall care to see that reverence and respect bee had to the Ministers." Furthermore, the commander was required to see that such rules as the preachers devised for the godly reformation of the crews should be enforced strictly and any "transgressours and contemners" should be severely punished.[32]

Madox took a high view of his duties and considered himself an apostolic missionary as well as the vicar of a floating parish. Before leaving Oxford he petitioned convocation to grant him a faculty "to preach the Word of God throughout the whole world." [33] Perhaps the Earl of Leicester, who as chancellor of the University had procured Madox' leave from All Souls, looked upon him as a pioneer who would pave the way for the establishment of a Protestant bulwark against the Catholics beyond the seas. Clearly Leicester had some great purpose in mind when he dictated the appointment of both Madox and Walker. They were no ordinary ship's chaplains. They enjoyed the favor of their bishops and received gifts from Sir Francis Drake. Before sailing, they both had an audience with the Queen. Leicester and Drake probably hoped that the ministers would return and preach a Protestant crusade to save the heathen world from the Catholics.

Madox had already distinguished himself as a preacher, and one notable sermon, delivered at Weymouth and Melcombe Regis, must have appealed particularly to Drake. Published in 1581 as *A Learned And A Godly Sermon, to be read of all men, but especially for all Marryners, Captaynes, and Passengers, which travall the Seas*, it is brief and to the point, full of salty idioms that show a familiarity with the sea. Among other good lessons, the sermon pointed out the folly of quarrels and dissensions which can bring a city as well as a ship to "a pitiful wreck." [34] Here, indeed, was a preacher that any commander might prize, for he knew the lessons of the sea as well as those of God. Walker was only a little behind Madox in attainments, and, if possible, exceeded him in zeal.

From the start, the voyage took on the air of a conventicle. On the day of sailing, Madox preached an eloquent sermon, on the deck of the flagship "Leicester," before Master Henry Ughtrede, mayor of Southampton, and other dignitaries who had come to see the expedition off. The chaplain brought credit to his patron, the mayor wrote to the Earl of Leicester, who must have been equally pleased at the mayor's added hope for the ships in this fleet: "I wish all the King of Spain, his gold, in their bellies to temper the pride of such a tyrant." [35] In their own way, the two parsons were also determined to humble the pride of His Most Catholic Majesty. At sea a religious atmosphere hovered over the ships. As in Frobisher's fleet, the watchword was a pious phrase: the challenging ship signaled, "If God be for us," and the others replied, "Who can be against us." Each day began and ended with prayer. Dice and cardplaying, swearing, and even vain talk were strictly forbidden.[36] To supply the place of these idle iniquities, common to seamen, Walker instituted religious discussion groups—a practice beloved of the Puritans—and is reported to have brought many souls to salvation.[37]

After so much had been done to insure the blessings of Providence, the Earl of Leicester must have been grievously puzzled at the results of the voyage, which proved one of the most miserable failures of the century. The fleet got no farther than the coast of Brazil, where quarrels between the captains and the appearance of a Spanish force led to the separation of the vessels, which then turned back to England. Before the fleet scattered they captured one prize, a small Spanish ship—manned by eighteen friars. Not even a hatred of papists could give them an excuse to keep this peaceful vessel; so, after robbing the friars of sugar and ginger, they let them go.[38] On the voyage home, John Walker died. Madox returned to a less eventful life in Oxford.

That God had especially reserved certain portions of

North America for the English, and hence had thwarted the Spanish and French in their efforts to push northward, was a belief fostered by Sir Humphrey Gilbert and his colleagues, leaders of the first expedition that made a serious effort to take possession of American lands for English colonization. Preachers were later to use this belief as an argument proving the manifest destiny of Englishmen to settle in the New World. Gilbert had a bold dream of neutralizing Spanish commercial and colonial power by opening up a Northwest Passage and establishing English colonies in the adjacent lands of the North American continent. Although a staunch Protestant himself, with an earnest desire to establish the Church of England in foreign parts, he found allies among certain loyal English Catholics. The leaders of these Catholics were Sir George Peckham and Sir Thomas Gerrard, who disliked Spain as heartily as Gilbert but hoped that a refuge for their coreligionists might be found abroad.[39] Gilbert's ill-organized and ill-fated expedition of 1583, which had for its purpose the establishment of an Anglican empire in North America, curiously had the support of violent Protestants and patriotic Catholics, who both emphasized a religious motive in their endeavors.

The high point of the expedition was reached when Gilbert sailed into St. John's harbor, Newfoundland, and formally took possession in the name of the Queen of England. The ceremony occurred on August 5, in the presence of a puzzled crowd of fishermen, of various nations, who had long regarded Newfoundland as common ground. The first item of Gilbert's proclamation asserted that henceforth the public exercise of religion should be according to the Church of England.

After some further exploration of possible sites for a colony on the coast of Nova Scotia, Gilbert sailed for England with the two ships remaining from the five with which he had set out. Off the Azores his own little vessel, the "Squirrel," foundered. Edward Hayes, captain of the surviving "Golden Hind," reported that, on the afternoon before the "Squirrel" was lost, "the Generall [Gilbert] sitting abaft with a booke in his hand, cried out unto us in the Hind (so oft as we did approch within hearing) We are as neere to heaven by sea as by land. Reiterating the same speech, well beseeming a souldier, resolute in Jesus Christ, as I can testifie he was." [40] A little afterward the "Squirrel" sank. Gilbert's piety exceeded his judgment as a leader, and his apologists had much to do to explain the failure.

Hayes's account of the expedition is notable for the ingenious way in which he set out to prove the benevolent hand of God in English enterprise in the northern latitudes, and at the same time tried to excuse the disasters which overtook Gilbert. His narrative displays the language and the sanctimonious quality of a sermon. The first portion is a demonstration of England's claims to the north part of America, with an assertion of God's obvious intention that the English were to colonize and Christianize it. Success, Hayes points out emphatically, is dependent upon the purity of the motives of the adventurers, who must be stirred by a zeal to save "poore infidels captived by the devill," as well as by a desire to relieve the poor of England and advance the interest of the nation.[41] The time is now ripe to garner the infidels to God and to bring that vast realm under the banners of Christ and Queen Elizabeth. Divine Providence is ready to bestow a blessing upon any Englishman of "a vertuous & heroycall minde" who undertakes this patriotic and godly adventure.

After such an assertion of God's interest in English colonization, Hayes had to account for Gilbert's misfortunes, because Gilbert was known for his personal piety, and the missionary motive in his expedition had been prominently set forth. Although we must "leave unto God" the complete understanding of the mystery, Hayes implies that "many ill-disposed people" in the fleet—including a villainous crew of cutthroat pirates—had much to do with the disaster. Furthermore, the leader lacked seamanship and common sense—qualities which even the Almighty recognized as necessary in a North Atlantic voyage. Thus the expedition had within itself the seeds of ruin, and Hayes warns his readers not to jump to any unwarranted conclusions and "misdeeme that God doth resist all attempts intended that way." [42] Richard Hakluyt, as a shrewd propagandist, knew the value of emphasizing the religious aspects of colonization, and perhaps his revision is responsible for the tone of Captain Hayes's relation, which he published in *The Principal Navigations*.

A harvest of heathen souls was not the only reward of colonization held out by Edward Hayes. He adroitly suggested that rich mines might also be found [43]—and fat lands that would bring wealth to their owners. The happy union of material prosperity and spiritual benefits made an argument believed to be irresistible; at any rate, this idea was set forth with even greater cogency by a second apology for Gilbert's voyage, G. P.'s *A True Reporte, Of the late discoueries, and possession, taken . . . of the New-found Landes: By . . . Sir Humfrey Gilbert Knight,* first published in 1583.[44] The author pictures the poor pagans thirsting after salvation, "as well gratefull to the Sauages, as gainfull to the Christians."[45] Smugly he reasons that the infidels' deliverances from Satan will be sufficient recompense for the loss of their tribal lands to godly Englishmen. Moreover, when the heathen have been taught to dress in Christian apparel, English clothiers will find in America a great vent for their goods, to the immense profit of artisans and merchants alike. Thus the labor of civilizing the Indians will not be lost, and all classes will share in a divine prosperity. The hope of profits so obsessed G. P. that he conveys the impression that Christianity is a merchantable commodity in great demand on the coast of Nova Scotia; his tract had the essential outlines of an argument that was to be further developed and often used by merchants and missionaries for generations to come.

That the discovery of a Northwest Passage to the Pacific would have an immense spiritual value was the belief earnestly held by Captain John Davis of Sandridge, an explorer of much experience and the author of works on geography and navigation. Like Drake and other west-country seamen, Davis had a genuine piety that manifested itself in both practice and theory. He believed he owed to a fervent prayer his rescue from destruction during an October storm encountered in 1591, in Thomas Cavendish's second voyage to the South Seas. Captain Davis and his men had yielded themselves to death, but, as a last comfort, Davis took a stiff drink of brandy and made a long prayer, concluding with a supplication to Christ to "shew us some mercifull signe of thy love and our preservation." Whereupon, reported one John Jane, his companion on the voyage, "before I went from him the Sunne shined cleere." [46] Because he attributed all the voyage's troubles to "our own offences against the divine Majesty," Davis exhorted his men to forget the vanities of this life so that they might find favor with God.[47] Later, when he came to write *The Worldes Hydrographical Discription* (1595), which had for its chief purpose proof of the existence of a northerly passage to the East Indies, he laid great stress on the religious aspects of the anticipated discovery. In a chapter enumerating advantages of that route to the Indies, he declares that "the benefits which may grow by this discovery are copious, and of two sorts—a benefit spirituall and a benefit corporall." Concerning the first, he quotes at length from Holy Writ to show the blessings to be derived from carrying out the scriptural injunction to spread the message of Christianity and "to multiply and increase the flocke of the faithfull." [48] Davis suggests that material success is dependent upon the sincere pursuance of missionary endeavor, and he concludes his treatise with the assertion that "it is impossible that any true English hart should be staied from willing contribution to the performance of this so excellent a discovery, the Lords and subjectes spirituall for the sole publication of Gods glorious gospell. And the Lords and subjectes temporal, for the renowne of their prince and glory of their nation." [49]

Further evidence of Davis' piety is found, of all places, in his excellent and popular treatise on navigation, *The Seamans Secrets,* probably first printed in 1594, in which he maintains that navigation is a divine science because it will make possible the spread of the word of God and the "blessed recouery of the forraine ofcastes from whence it hath pleased his diuine Maiestie as yet to detayne the brightnes of his glorie." [50] With a proper care for good seamanship on the part of the English, Davis believes that Protestant Christianity can be spread to the ends of the earth and Catholic Spain may be driven back to the Iberian Peninsula. These holy and patriotic objectives, in his opinion, are inseparable and equally desirable.

Davis was the friend of Sir Humphrey Gilbert and his brother Adrian, of Sir Walter Raleigh, and of the mathematician John Dee. In his diary Dee mentions secret conferences between Davis, Adrian Gilbert, himself, and Sir Francis Walsingham, at which they discussed proposed explorations for the Northwest Passage.[51] Dee, too, was interested in the propagation of the gospel among the infidels, and Walsingham was committed to incessant hostility to Spain. We can be certain, therefore, that these secret conferences dealt with high matters of state and religion.

Even Raleigh, least religious of the great Elizabethan adventurers, seems to have been convinced of the value of evangelizing the heathen. A manuscript attributed to him, entitled "Of the Voyage for Guiana," gives the greatest emphasis to arguments for converting "infinite nombers of soules" to Protestant Christianity so that "the intollerable tiranny of the Spaniards" might be ended and the "mouthes of the Romish Catholickes" might be stopped.[52] The natives of Guiana, the author of the manuscript goes on to say, can be made one of the most potent means of harassing Spain if Englishmen will cultivate their friendship and bring them to the obedience of the gospel.[53] To this end, missionaries should be sent among the Guianans, but Raleigh warns that the refusal of the infidels to accept Christianity immediately should not be made an excuse for laying waste their land with the sword.[54] Raleigh's enlightened attitude was not accepted unanimously by his contemporaries, who frequently produced texts from the Old Testament to prove the right of followers of the true Jehovah to take by force the lands of the Canaanites.

Emphasis upon religion as a motive of colonization and as a factor in success at sea was accentuated as the sixteenth century drew toward a close. Perhaps the development of Puritan ideas may partially account for the increasing religious note, but that factor is not obvious. Puritans were hardly more concerned about religious exercises than were others of less precise natures. For example, the Earl of Cumberland, more famous for privateering than for Puritanism, on a voyage to Puerto Rico, in 1596, reprimanded severely a young gallant for reading *Orlando Furioso* during morning prayers. As the chaplain, one Dr. Layfield, reports the incident, his Lordship rebuked the irreverent youth before the entire ship's company, "and having told him that we might looke that God would serve us accordingly, if we served not him better," warned that for a second offense "he would cast his Booke over-boord, and turne himselfe out of the ship." [55] Special religious observances marked the expedition against Cadiz in 1596, although its leaders were anything but precisians. They included a political Puritan in the person of the Earl of Essex, Catholics in Lord Admiral Sir Charles Howard and Sir Thomas Howard, and a freethinker in Sir Walter Raleigh. An old and experienced sea captain, John Young, drew up rules of discipline for the voyage, forbidding mariners and soldiers to dispute about religion except to be relieved of doubts—in which case they were ordered to consult a chaplain. The expedition was well equipped with chaplains, for Essex alone had four, the Lord Admiral three, and Raleigh, Sir Thomas Howard, and the Earl of Sussex one each. Whatever the individual faith of the leaders might be, the chaplains were ministers whose theology was approved by the Established Church. Prayers were said throughout the fleet twice a day, and Queen Elizabeth herself is said to have written a special prayer for these occasions. [56]

In this as in other expeditions, chaplains were concerned with morale as well as with morals and religion. In an age which universally accepted supernatural religion, it is easy to understand the influence that preachers could exert upon sailors, ever a superstitious group. Believing as they did in the value of intercessory prayer, Elizabethan seamen felt infinitely more secure in times of crisis if they knew that the supplications of holy men were reaching the throne of an all-powerful deity. Moreover, the preachers constantly stressed practical doctrines that every commander applauded: obedience, diligence, sobriety, courage, and all the kindred virtues. Thus a preacher might prove an exceedingly useful officer in any ship's company. The preacher's influence, however, was not invariably pleasing to the authorities. Occasionally he cautioned restraint against too enthusiastic piracy, and sometimes sided with the crew in threatened mutinies. For instance, the chaplain John Cartwright was charged with responsibility for the failure of Captain George Weymouth's expedition in 1602 in search of the Northwest Passage, because he helped persuade officers and crew to turn back and give up the voyage.[57] On the whole, however, preachers and the religion they expounded exerted a powerful influence in the furtherance of Elizabethan maritime enterprise.

The sixteenth century was still an age of faith, and the Bible had never before held so important a place in the lives of ordinary men. With the Puritans' increasing emphasis upon the individual's duty of searching the Scriptures for guidance in everyday affairs of life, it is not surprising that the impact of religion should have been felt even among corsairs and buccaneers, who smote the papist Spaniards, enriched themselves, and first carried the name of England and the Protestant Jehovah to the heathen.

Although the missionary movement was not yet to become a great factor in English expansion—as it did in the nineteenth century—the constant repetition of the evangelical theme helped to give maritime enterprise in Elizabeth's reign a color of godly endeavor. Whether intended as propaganda or not, the often-stated belief in the duty of Englishmen to carry their religion to foreign parts gained the favor of the clergy and helped to win the support of pious folk for many an expedition, even some of doubtful merit. If the direct results of all this religious talk were not immediately obvious, the psychological effect upon English public opinion was immensely important. Englishmen learned that they had a destiny on the seas, and they came to believe that God himself would approve and bless their enterprises.

CHAPTER TWO

Richard Hakluyt:

Preacher and Imperialist

I F , I N the shadow world of departed spirits, British explorers, adventurers, and colonizers meet in a ghostly geographical society, their permanent secretary is Richard Hakluyt, preacher, sometime student of Christ Church in Oxford. And the minutes of those meetings, in their matter-of-fact way, will manage to convey the idea that the lands of the western world and the islands in tropic seas were especially reserved for the English nation, to be colonized by Englishmen and Christianized for the Protestant Jehovah. For Richard Hakluyt had a vision and a mission. His life was consecrated to the great task of arousing his countrymen to opportunities overseas and the duty of Englishmen to seize vast sleeping empires for their sovereign and their God. The quiet labors of this man of religion exerted a greater influence on English expansion than the deeds of any other single Englishman of the sixteenth century.[1]

We usually think of Hakluyt as editor and compiler

33

of *The Principal Navigations,* better known as the *Voyages.*
Since the publication of George B. Parks's fine biography,
however, we have become aware of Hakluyt's tremendous
labors for the science of geography and his propaganda for
colonial expansion. But not yet have we fully appreciated
Hakluyt the preacher, the zealot who made of colonial expansion a religion and equated the maritime enterprise of
Englishmen with the divine plan of the universe. It is
nevertheless true that religion was the mainspring of much
of Hakluyt's endeavor, and his religious zeal, combined
with sound sense and scientific learning, increased his prestige and influence with his contemporaries.

In the twentieth century we find it too easy to dismiss the
religious utterances of dwellers in an earlier century as
cant, or, at best, as a conventionality. We are prone to
evaluate men of the sixteenth century in terms of our own
time. And we forget that practical, scientific observers like
Richard Hakluyt were not the philosophic rationalists they
would be today. As the Elizabethan adventurers believed
in a supernatural being who controlled their destinies and
commanded their worship, so Hakluyt devoutly adhered
to the same faith, with an added professional obligation to
spread the gospel. The religious motive in exploration and
colonization, which he so often puts forward in his own
writings, represented a sincere and profound belief. If it
proved also a telling argument—as it undoubtedly did—
that fact is simply one more proof of the religious nature of
the sixteenth and early seventeenth centuries.

While still a student of Westminster School, young
Hakluyt underwent a mystical conversion to the science of

geography. He himself vividly describes the experience which set him on the path to the dual vocation of geographer and preacher. "I do remember that being a youth, and one of her Majesties scholars at Westminster that fruitfull nurserie," he remarks in an epistle dedicating the 1589 edition of *The Principal Navigations* to Sir Francis Walsingham, "it was my happe to visit the chamber of M. Richard Hakluyt my cosin, a Gentleman of the Middle Temple, well knowen unto you, at a time when I found lying open upon his boord certeine bookes of Cosmographie, with an universall Mappe: he seeing me somewhat curious in the view therof, began to instruct my ignorance, by shewing me the division of the earth into three parts after the olde account, and then according to the latter, & better distribution, into more: he pointed with his wand to all the knowen Seas, Gulfs, Bayes, Straightes, Capes, Rivers, Empires, Kingdomes, Dukedomes, and Territories of each part, with declaration also of their speciall commodities, & particular wants, which by the benefit of traffike, & entercourse of merchants, are plentifully supplied. From the Mappe he brought me to the Bible, and turning to the 107 Psalme, directed mee to the 23 & 24 verses, where I read, that they which go downe to the sea in ships, and occupy by the great waters, they see the works of the Lord, and his woonders in the deepe, &c. Which words of the Prophet together with my cousins discourse (things of high and rare delight to my yong nature) tooke in me so deepe an impression, that I constantly resolved, if ever I were preferred to the University, where better time, and more convenient place might be ministred for these studies, I would by Gods assistance prosecute that knowledge and kinde of literature, the doores whereof (after a sort) were so happily opened before me." [2] The combination of secular and religious interests demonstrated in Hakluyt's "call" to study geography continued throughout his life.

At Christ Church, Oxford, where Hakluyt proceeded to the bachelor's degree in 1574 and the master's in 1577, he had an opportunity for studies that fitted him for his twofold career, but he is careful to note that his geographical reading came only after the "exercises of duety first performed." [3] Although the formal university curriculum as yet offered little that an inquiring young man of a scientific turn of mind would find useful, at both universities there were learned men who had been stirred by the new science, and at Oxford Hakluyt met kindred spirits who aided him in his scientific studies. After he had finished his formal training and taken holy orders, he gave public lectures in cosmography and boasts that he was the first publicly to compare the old and the new science of geography and to display the reformed maps, globes, and "other instruments of this Art for demonstration in the common schooles, to the singular pleasure, and generall contentment of my auditory." [4] Thus, while Hakluyt was learning the skill of the preacher, he was also becoming the instructor of others who would teach the new cosmographical sciences.

Hakluyt was not the only young clerk of Oxford who came under the spell of the new science. At Balliol College in the sixties, William Barlow, son of the Bishop of Chichester, learned what he could about navigation and perhaps went to sea. Later, when he had become a church dignitary, first as treasurer of the Cathedral of Lichfield and afterward as archdeacon of Salisbury, he turned his talents to cosmography and navigation, but not without explaining the high religious purpose of these studies. In the dedication to the Earl of Essex of *The Navigators Supply* (1597), an excellent textbook for sailors, Barlow declares that skill in navigation is necessary "to carrie the sound of the Gospell, as the band of loue, into all dispersed Islands and out-Angles of the world." [5] Hence he is devoting his knowledge and skill to that worthy science, as a divine instrument of salvation for untold thousands of heathen. On the title-page of his book he printed the same text from the 107th Psalm that had been instrumental in converting Hakluyt to cosmography.

Another member of the group of youthful Oxford clergymen, enamored of the study of science and cosmography, was Hakluyt's friend Philip Jones, a preacher from the seaport of Bristol, who produced a manual designed to teach travelers how to make useful and accurate observations abroad. The little book was translated from Albertus Meierus as *Certaine briefe and speciall Instructions* (1589). In the dedication to Sir Francis Drake, Jones says the translation was suggested by Hakluyt, "a man of incredible deuotion towarde your selfe, and of speciall carefulnesse for the good of our Nation." Jones, like any good west-country preacher, wishes success to Drake's expedition against the Spaniards and hopes that it may be "the terror of Antichrist, the comfort of the Church, the honour of our Prince, the renowne of our kingdome, and the immortality of your owne name."

37

Another ecclesiastical geographer of Oxford whom Hakluyt knew and may have influenced was George Abbot, son of a clothworker of Guildford, who took his B.A. at Balliol in 1582, and in 1611 became Archbishop of Canterbury. While master of University College, Abbot published a syllabus of geography, entitled *A Briefe Description Of The whole worlde* (1599), a work so popular that it went through eight editions by 1636. About the time that he printed his geography, Abbot also completed *An Exposition Vpon The Prophet Jonah* (1600), consisting of thirty sermons on the recalcitrant missionary to Nineveh. In these lectures the ecclesiastic demonstrated both geographical and theological learning, and revealed the bias against Spanish Catholicism that later, when he was Archbishop of Canterbury, characterized his foreign policy. Abbot, a Protestant zealot, believed the safety of England demanded the checking by Protestants of the imperial expansion of Spain. That political tenet helps to explain his interest in geographical exploration and colonization, and the favor he showed Hakluyt, Samuel Purchas, and other pious advocates of expansion abroad.

Oxford clergymen, represented by men like Barlow, Jones, Hakluyt, and Abbot, composed an influential group who realized, before the end of the sixteenth century, that England's destiny required expansion beyond the seas. All England knew that Spain was a constant threat to the island's security, but the conservatives, headed by Lord Burleigh, urged the nation to play safe, keep the peace, and out-trade Spain in diplomatic bargaining. Meanwhile the more vigorous imperialists, led by Walsingham, Essex,

Raleigh, and other daring spirits, urged an attack on Spain's colonial empire. In this conflict the preachers wielded an increasing influence, and Hakluyt and his colleagues of the cloth played an important part in winning public opinion to favor an anti-Spanish imperialism. Some of ·the Oxford clergy of Hakluyt's acquaintance were tinged with Puritanism, but hatred of Spain was not confined to Puritans. Conservative Anglicans, and even English Catholics, likewise feared Spain, and the clergy generally, regardless of their particular sectarian slant, fell in with the imperialists. For them Hakluyt became the chief spokesman and Abbot a powerful ecclesiastical protagonist.

Richard Hakluyt, it is well to remember, throughout his career was an active preacher, conscious of the responsibility of his calling and diligent in the performance of his religious duties. Unlike some of the "literary clergy" of the nineteenth century, he did not use ecclesiastical appointments merely as a convenient means to a secular end. Indeed, his labors for exploration and colonization were a complementary part of his religious career, and he utilized opportunities incidental to either profession for the mutual benefit of both.

Hakluyt's first important ecclesiastical post was that of chaplain to Sir Edward Stafford, ambassador to France. With some reluctance, apparently, he gave up a project to go with Sir Humphrey Gilbert's expedition to the New World, and in the autumn of 1583 went instead to France, where he served for the next five years, with occasional visits to England. During this time he made numerous contacts with learned men, talked to many sailors, pored over the maps of the best geographers of Europe, became the confidant and religious adviser of French Protestants, contemplated the threat of Catholic Spain, and meditated upon a plan to promote the evangelization of the Indians and the settlement of English Protestants beyond the wide seas.

Meanwhile Queen Elizabeth gave him a mandate to the chapter of Bristol Cathedral for the next vacant prebend, to which he was admitted sometime before 1587.[6] Two years after his return from France he also became rector of Wetheringsett, in Suffolk, and took up his long residence there as an earnest country parson, performing all his parish duties without a curate. For more than a decade he received no further preferment, but in 1602 he was admitted to a prebend in Westminster Abbey, and two years afterward Sir Robert Cecil, who had made him his personal chaplain, procured for him an appointment as chaplain of the Savoy in London. Later in life he was made canon of St. Augustine's Cathedral, in Bristol, and had the living of Gedney, in Lincolnshire. In Westminster Abbey he held various responsible offices, serving as archdeacon in 1603–4, steward of the chapter in 1607–8, and treasurer in 1614–15.[7] All this time he continued to perform the duties of his old parish at Wetheringsett. The several pluralities, which came late, were in recognition of his public services; but, even so, they were not sinecures and entailed a considerable amount of work. There is no indication that the parson ever shirked his ecclesiastical tasks or felt that his service to the state was more important than his obligations to the church. Indeed, in Hakluyt's own mind, all his labors, secular and strictly religious, tended equally to the glory of God.

Though a moderate man without the least taint of the fanaticism which characterized the later Puritans, inevitably Hakluyt cast his lot with the Puritan party, a political group that numbered among its leaders Sir Philip Sidney, the Earl of Leicester, Sir Francis Walsingham, and Sir Walter Raleigh. More political than sectarian in motivation, these men were chiefly concerned with establishing the Protestant interest against the power of Catholic Spain. Hakluyt found their objectives congenial to his own beliefs. That the spread of Spanish Catholicism threatened the very existence of England was one of his fundamental tenets and helps to explain the fervor with which he carried on his crusade for colonization in the New World.

In one of the earliest pieces to survive from Hakluyt's pen, "A Discourse of the Commodity of the Taking of the Straight of Magellanus," dated 1580 and preserved in manuscript among the state papers, he argues the grave peril to Europe if Spain is permitted to control Portugal and take over all of the East and West Indies.[8] To prevent such a catastrophe, he urges three measures: fortification and garrisoning of each end of the Straits of Magellan, capture and fortification of Cape St. Vincent in Brazil, and the development of the northeastern trade routes to Russia and, it was hoped, to Cathay. To prevent immediate trouble with Spain, Hakluyt suggests, with shrewd cunning, that one Clerke, a pirate, might be induced to establish a stronghold at the Straits as if for himself, without the countenance of the English nation. Garrisoning the forts might also become a Christian and humanitarian enterprise if Indians enslaved by the Spaniards could be rescued and sent to people that region, along with a few English convicts, men and women, who could win their freedom by emigrating. Nothing came of this bold scheme, but Hakluyt's arguments that permanent English colonies and adequate naval bases were essential for protection against Spain demonstrated his developing sense of geopolitics.

Contacts with French Huguenots during his service as chaplain to the ambassador accentuated an innate suspicion of Catholics in general. The memory of the Massacre of St. Bartholomew's Day was still bitter in the minds of French Protestants, and Hakluyt listened sympathetically to their stories of persecution. As he talked with his coreligionists and with geographers, the impression grew that the time had come for Protestantism to build an empire beyond the seas. England as the greatest Protestant power had an obligation to take the leadership. Already, prominent Puritans at home were urging such action upon the government, and Hakluyt quickly became a zealot for this cause.

The choice of Sir Philip Sidney—one of the noblest protagonists of the reformed religion—as the patron of Hakluyt's first compilation, the *Divers Voyages* (1582), was significant of the editor's purpose. The opening sentence of the dedication is a tactful rebuke to Englishmen for allowing Spain and Portugal to gobble up the New World, but the compiler finds consolation in Portugal's downfall and the weaknesses which Drake and others had discovered in Spain's defenses. He points out that a vast region northward from Florida now lies open, "unplanted by Christians." By citing the example of a noble Portuguese who wished to use all his substance in sending settlers "for the inhabiting of those countries, and reducing those gentile people to christianitie," the editor tries to shame his countrymen into recognizing their own duty. Here, again, Hakluyt urges the humanitarian value of colonization: English prisons are crowded with men and women, convicted of petty offenses, who ask only an opportunity to become honest and useful citizens in a new land. Failure of the English to establish a foothold abroad, the editor insists, has come from "a preposterous desire of seeking rather gaine then God's glorie." Actually, material rewards will come incidentally when men begin to put God first, says Hakluyt the preacher. Previously, "wee forgotte, that Godliness is great riches, and that if we first seeke the kingdome of God, al other thinges will be given unto us." With earnest sincerity the parson urges the advancement of Christianity as a necessary policy in statecraft; neglect to spread the gospel will result in the failure of English enterprise, as the Spaniards have already failed in many ventures because their efforts at converting the infidels have been hollow pretenses.

The beliefs expressed by Hakluyt in his dedication to Sidney were reiterated and elaborated at every opportunity during the rest of his career. These ideas, common enough in the religious thinking of the day, gained new force by reason of Hakluyt's advocacy and helped a little later to influence the directors of the East India and Virginia companies.

A state paper, prepared by Hakluyt and presented in person to the Queen in 1584, set forth with great detail his views on the colonial enterprise then being pushed by Raleigh. The document, conventionally abbreviated in title to the *Discourse of Western Planting*,[9] was prepared at the request of Raleigh himself and was designed to offer convincing reasons to Her Majesty for royal support of colonies in America, and in particular of Raleigh's infant colony just planted on the coast of North Carolina. Already Hakluyt had the confidence of Walsingham, as well as of Raleigh, and the two hoped to use the geographer's knowledge and reasoning, both religious and secular, in persuading the Queen of the soundness of this oblique attack on Spain. Seven years earlier Sir Humphrey Gilbert had presented the Queen with a paper describing "How Her Majesty may annoy the King of Spain," but no notice had been taken of his plan. Now Hakluyt, with the encouragement of influential men in the government, outlined a scheme by which Elizabeth might not only "annoy" but could "bringe kinge Phillippe from his high Throne, and make him equal to the Princes his neighbours."

In essence, the scheme provided for the fortification of bases to threaten the West Indies, the planting of colonies on the American coast north of Florida, and the securing of the Northwest Passage to the East. Much of the argument is based on religious grounds, with careful emphasis upon the dangers of popery and a description of the cruelties of the Spanish churchmen in the New World. By striking a blow for Protestantism and for England, the Queen would incidentally win the sources of the vast wealth in gold and silver which had previously gone to enrich the coffers of His Majesty of Spain.

The *Discourse of Western Planting* begins like a sermon, and throughout its twenty-one chapters the author never forgets his holy vocation, albeit his advice could not have been more practical had it come from the most calculating worldling. The first chapter enlarges upon the thesis that the western discoveries have provided a heaven-sent opportunity for the spread of the gospel, "whereunto the Princes of the refourmed Relligion are chefely bounde"— among whom Queen Elizabeth is the foremost. Because English sovereigns have the title of defenders of the faith, Hakluyt maintains, "they are not onely chardged to mayne-teyne and patronize the faithe of Christe, but also to inlarge and advaunce the same. Neither oughte this to be their laste worke but rather the principall and chefe of all others." [10] It will not be sufficient merely to send missionaries to the infidels of America, as Spanish friars went to Florida only to meet death; on the contrary, the fulfillment of God's injunctions requires the settlement of colonies among the savages. Though preachers had gone out with Frobisher, Drake, and Fenton, Englishmen cannot yet boast of any single infidel converted. But God "hath his tyme for all men," and England's time for evangelical enterprise is at hand.

One argument that Hakluyt used in the same chapter must have appealed to the shrewd Queen. Because preachers at home have not enough to do and are prone to idleness, they stir up strife, grow contentious about ceremonies, and are "alwayes coyninge of new opynions." But if they were sent abroad with colonists, they would be too busy about the Lord's work to worry over trifling matters, and "in reducing the Savages to the chefe principles of our faiths, will become less contentious, and be contented with the truthe in Relligion alreadie established by aucthoritie." The Queen, faced with the rising spirit of dissension among the clergy, must have read these words with sympathetic attention. Nothing could give a clearer notion of Hakluyt's own attitude toward theological Puritanism. Though he was an active spokesman for policies of the Puritan political group, he had no sympathy with opponents of the church already established by "aucthoritie." He was a common sense "middle-of-the-roader," and the Queen's own *via media* suited him precisely.

The curtailment of the liberties of English merchants and the limitations upon English trade, especially in the Spanish dominions, "where our men are dryven to flinge their bibles and prayer bookes into the sea, and to forsweare and renownce their Relligion and conscience," is the theme of the second chapter. The necessity of trading with Spain, where merchants must risk the punishments of the Inquisition or endanger their immortal souls, will be ended when the opportunities for expansion overseas are realized. Specific details of the advantages of this expansion and the means of attaining these happy ends make up the rest of Hakluyt's treatise. He paints a gorgeous picture of the commodities of the Indies, ready for Englishmen to grasp, and in his careful way he becomes almost ecstatic over the plenitude of soap ashes and fish in Newfoundland. When these new areas of settlement and trade come under the flag of England, unemployment will disappear, and idle men, who now grow mutinous and seek alterations

in the state, will no longer be burdensome to the common-
wealth. Into his paper, for the eyes of the Queen, Hakluyt
adroitly insinuates the idea that the safety of both church
and state demands expansion and maritime development.

A few good fortifications in the Florida region to serve
as naval bases for operations against New Spain would give
the English a great military advantage, Hakluyt argues.
The Spanish treasure fleets could be intercepted, and the
Indies would be at the mercy of English ships stationed
within easy striking distance. Moreover, in the north parts
of New Spain are valiant Indians, who could be armed to
wage guerrilla warfare against the Spaniards, as the Spaniards themselves have armed Irish rebels to worry the English. The elimination of the sources of Spanish wealth is
one aim of Hakluyt's proposals. In an impassioned appeal,
he urges the Queen to remember how Spanish gold has
corrupted all Europe, how hired assassins endanger the
lives of Protestant princes, how Spanish subsidies foster
papist seminaries for renegade Englishmen, and how their
bribes spread disaffection among her subjects.[11] To arouse
the Queen to a proper horror of Spain, he describes atrocities committed on the hapless Indians and quotes in proof
some of the most colorful and gruesome passages from
Bartolomé de las Casas.

Spain's asserted title to the western world, based on the
donation of Pope Alexander VI, Hakluyt demolishes with
arguments from the Scriptures, from the church fathers,
and from common sense; then, on the basis of Sebastian
Cabot's voyages of discovery during the reign of Henry
VII, he demonstrates Elizabeth's claim to all the north

47

part of America. The treatise finally builds up to a climax with a statement of twenty-three reasons why Her Majesty ought to take in hand western discovery and colonization.[12] Among the motives which Hakluyt hoped would appeal to the Queen were the assured benefits to the merchant marine and the navy, the general increase in the prosperity of the commercial and artisan classes, and especially the anticipated profits of the cloth trade when native Americans should be taught to wear Christian raiment. Characteristic of Hakluyt's practical sense was a concluding chapter of memoranda "of some thinges to be prepared for the voyadge." Not forgotten in this list of essentials were "one or twoo preachers," Bibles and service books, and works describing the discovery and conquest of the East and West Indies—these last "to kepe men occupied from worse cogitations, and to raise their myndes to courage and highe enterprizes and to make them lesse careles for the better shonnynge of common daungers."[13] Lastly, as if, after all his warnings, the directors of voyages might forget the hazards of Catholic Spain, Hakluyt adds a note of advice that "this general rule were good to be observed that no man be chosen that is knowen to be a papiste for the speciall inclynation they have of favour to the kinge of Spaine."[14] Thus, with piety, learning, logic, and practical statesmanship, Richard Hakluyt persuaded his sovereign of the value of expansion to the west. Of the various motives that prompted him, none was stronger than his zeal for the Protestant faith, with its corollary hostility to Catholic Spain.

Along with the *Discourse of Western Planting*, Hakluyt

also presented to Queen Elizabeth a commentary, in Latin, on Aristotle's *Politics;* this document has perished. Whether he invoked the authority of Aristotle in support of colonial expansion and the theories of statecraft set forth in the *Discourse,* we can only guess, but, from what we know of Hakluyt's singleness of purpose, we may surmise that he did.

To further the policies outlined in the *Discourse* became the fixed goal of Hakluyt's endeavors during the rest of his life. In the program presented to the Queen he detailed more fully than elsewhere in his writings his beliefs in the aims and purposes of expansion, but in all of his succeeding works he constantly reiterated these doctrines.

Hostile as Hakluyt was to Spain, he realized that a frontal attack on the southern dominions already occupied by the Spaniards stood less chance of success than the gradual occupation of the North American mainland. He hoped that the English could compass the downfall of Spain by this flanking movement, without precipitating immediate hostilities which might be disastrous. Furthermore, he was shrewd enough to know that he had to avoid antagonizing the cautious faction of Lord Burleigh, who followed a policy of pacification until the outbreak of open war with Spain. With more than a little tact, therefore, the wise propagandist set to work to demonstrate the value of North America and the justice of England's claims to that region. He even insisted that these claims did not conflict with the *de facto* rights of Spain. So skilful was his propaganda that he openly worked for the bolder expansionists and at the same time retained the confidence of Burleigh, and later enjoyed the patronage and support of Burleigh's son, Sir Robert Cecil, who, despite a distaste for the Spaniards, was inclined to follow the conciliatory policies of his father.

Through his friendship with influential Huguenots during his residence in France, Hakluyt brought to light a manuscript of René de Laudonnière—who had led a Huguenot expedition to Florida—and published it at his own expense as *L'histoire notable de la Floride* (Paris, 1586). This book, significantly, was dedicated to Raleigh, then the most vigorous leader of the colonial movement. A year later Hakluyt translated the book as *A Notable Historie Containing foure voyages made by Certayne French Captaynes vnto Florida* (1587). The dedicatory letter congratulates Raleigh on his zeal to establish colonies in Virginia and finds encouragement in the measures taken to insure the blessing of God on the enterprise. The pursuit of mere transitory gain is futile, Hakluyt observes, and too few voyagers heretofore have understood that they must seek "the glorie of God and the saving of the soules of the poore & blinded infidels." He has heard that Raleigh accordingly intends shortly to send "some such good Churchmen thither, as may truely saie with the Apostle to the Savages, We seeke not yours but you." That news, says the writer, is a "great Comfort of the successe of this your action," and he is certain that the Lord will bless the infant colony.[15] After thus assuring Raleigh of divine approval, Hakluyt quickly points out that a hundred men can now accomplish more in settling Virginia than a thousand Englishmen can achieve in Ireland; he has statistics of Portuguese colonial schemes to prove his statements. Moreover, the demobilization of soldiers returning from the Low Countries, with the consequent unemployment, offers an opportunity to recruit colonists of military skill.

The narrative of the experiences of the Huguenot settlers on the South Atlantic coast, the translator hopes, will stir the blood of Englishmen against the Spaniards, while the description of the fruitfulness of the land will arouse their desire to seize the country before Spain can gain possession of the entire region. The work gives a suggestion of Spanish weakness and closes with an account of French retaliation for the slaughter of Jean Ribaut's men near St. Augustine.[16] If Englishmen now take possession of the deserted country, the translator reasons, they will perform a Christian service for French Protestant refugees and, at the same stroke, win an empire that promises great riches.

During the critical times preceding the attack of the Spanish Armada in 1588, Hakluyt was employed as a confidential messenger between Sir Edward Stafford and Lord Burleigh. Some of the secret dispatches that he carried contained news of the preparations of the Armada and of political movements in France.[17] But, even in this crisis, he had time for geographical studies and busied himself with the final editorial preparation of his great compilation, *The Principall Navigations, Voiages And Discoveries Of The English nation, made by Sea or ouer Land,* which he brought out in 1589 with a dedication to Sir Francis Walsingham, that inveterate enemy of Spain, whose own hopes for an English empire overseas Hakluyt had long shared. For years preceding the appearance of the work, Hakluyt had been gathering material, verifying evidence, checking data, and translating foreign documents. During these years he had also encouraged other editors and translators to bring to light significant travel narratives, some of which he incorporated in his own collection. The success of the volume was immediate; mariners, merchants, and promoters read the narratives of exploration and trade and were stirred to go and do likewise. That was the effect that Hakluyt had intended. He looked forward to the day when Englishmen would be moved to settle in the great wastes and carry their religion and trade to the uttermost parts of the earth. As he prophesied to Walsingham, eventually Englishmen would take, even to Japan and the Philippines, "the incomparable treasure of the trueth of Christianity, and of the Gospell, while we use and exercise common trade with their marchants." [18]

In the decade after the first publication of *The Principal Navigations*, the compiler continued to collect material for a second edition, and in 1598 brought out the first of three great folio volumes, dedicated to Charles Howard, the Lord Admiral. Perhaps in deference to Howard's Catholic faith, Hakluyt said little, in the dedication, about religious motives, but he could not forbear mentioning ways in which Howard had previously humbled the Spaniards. In the two following years, he published the second and third volumes, both dedicated to Sir Robert Cecil, whom he flattered for his wisdom in colonial projects. As if conscious of a great message that he had to convey, Hakluyt proudly signed himself "Preacher" on the title-pages and the dedications of the last two volumes. The dedication of the 1599 volume makes a vigorous plea for the renewal of efforts to settle Virginia—this time at government expense. All the familiar arguments are rehearsed, as Hakluyt urges upon Mr. Secretary Cecil the advantages of a plan whereby Her Majesty could "increase her dominions, enrich her cofers, and reduce many Pagans to the faith of Christ." [19]

The magnificent scope of *The Principal Navigations* and its immense appeal to seafaring Englishmen have often been described. For a century after publication, the work exerted upon English imaginations an influence that exceeded even the compiler's dreams. It quickly found a place beside Foxe's *Book of Martyrs* and the King James version of the Bible, as reading deemed necessary to all good Englishmen. Indeed, the East India Company, in enumerating equipment regarded as essential to its ships, decreed that these three works were indispensable. With such a library, Protestant traders and mariners were prepared to deal with most of the problems of this world and the next. Perhaps the most important contribution of *The Principal Navigations*, even to contemporaries, was not the geographical data supplied but the stimulation that Englishmen received from the recital of their own maritime prowess. No other work did so much to confirm in the national consciousness the belief that England was by destiny the first seapower of the world, and certainly none more zealously advanced the doctrine that England's future prosperity lay in colonial expansion and the subjection of alien races to English religion and culture.

Laborious as were Hakluyt's efforts as an editor and a

compiler, he also had time to serve as a consultant on geography and colonization, and was active in various projects for trade and expansion. In 1597, after news of Raleigh's expedition to Guiana had excited interest in the valley of the Orinoco, Sir Robert Cecil discussed with him the suitability of that region for English settlers. It was a tribute to Hakluyt's reputation for scientific accuracy and honesty that Cecil consulted the man who had previously favored Raleigh's schemes, for Cecil had no love for Raleigh. Hakluyt, on his part, testifies to Cecil's own geographical knowledge and fairness in considering the project.[20] In 1599 Hakluyt attended the meeting which resulted in the organization of the East India Company, and for years was a technical consultant of that company. In 1603, he was instrumental in persuading a group of Bristol merchants to subsidize Martin Pring's voyage of discovery in New England waters. In 1606 he was one of the four London patentees in the first Virginia Company. Indeed, on November 21 of that year he received a dispensation, along with the Reverend Robert Hunter of Heathfield in Sussex, to go to Virginia, to "perform the ministry and preaching of God's word in those parts." [21] Although something prevented Hakluyt from proceeding to Virginia with the first settlers, he nevertheless invested £21 in the enterprise.[22] For the rest of his life he was devoted to the interest of the Virginia Company.[23] Finally, in 1612 he was a charter member of the Northwest Passage Company. By precept and example he sought to teach his countrymen the value and the profit of overseas enterprise.

Hakluyt neglected no opportunity to demonstrate England's rights to trade where she pleased and to colonize where expediency dictated. Soon after Hugo Grotius published his *Mare liberum* in 1608, Hakluyt translated it into English. The arguments that proved Dutch rights to the freedom of the seas and the privilege of trading in the East Indies were equally useful in proving England's claims. But the translation was never published, partly, one authority thinks, because England was at that time invoking an argument of a closed sea against the Dutch.[24]

To the end of his days, the editor and geographer continued his campaign to stir the English public to a realization of the necessity of expansion overseas as a counterweight to the Spanish empire. There is reason to believe that he is the author of two brief state papers—prepared in 1613, three years before his death—which defined the limitation of Spanish rights in the New World. One paper, entitled "The true Limites of all the Countries and Provinces at this present actually possessed by ye Spaniards and Portugals in the West Indies," once again proved to English satisfaction that Spain had no genuine claim to the northern part of the American continent. The second paper, which bore the caption, "Whether an Englishman may trade with the West Indies, with certain answers to the Popes Bull," invoked the law of nature and of nations to show that Englishmen might trade in the very center of the Spanish dominions without violating any legal or moral rights of the Spaniards.[25]

When Hakluyt died, in 1616, he was buried in Westminster Abbey, where in his late years he had performed many religious duties. It was fitting that he should rest among the great men of the nation that he sought to magnify into an empire. But worldly glory and chauvinistic pride were not his motives in advancing the cause of expansion. Hakluyt sincerely believed that imperial achievement was a part of the divine plan and that it was God's own command for English Protestants to go forth and people the earth. So firmly did he hold to this belief and so sensible and convincing were his arguments that apprentices, merchants, plain citizens, speculators, noblemen, ecclesiastics, and great statesmen were converted to his doctrine. After his time it was easier to persuade Englishmen of their destiny outside the little island girt by its silver sea. His scientific learning, common sense, honesty, piety, and prestige combined to lend weight to his arguments against the narrow conservatism that his countrymen had inherited from the past. Thanks to him, investors in colonial stock companies could take comfort in the realization that, while they sought fat profits, they might also contribute to a high moral cause. Imbued with religious and patriotic zeal, Richard Hakluyt became the first great—and successful—Apostle of Empire. Well did he deserve the praise with which Michael Drayton concluded his "Ode to the Virginian Voyage":

> *Thy Voyages attend,*
> *Industrious Hackluit,*
> *Whose reading shall inflame*
> *Men to seek fame,*
> *And much commend*
> *To after-times thy wit.*

CHAPTER THREE

Jehovah's Blessing

on the Eastern Trade

WHEN the English clergy thought of the New
World, they dreamed of a vast Protestant empire
and thousands of heathen who might be won to Jehovah
and taught a proper hostility to Catholic Spain; but when
they contemplated the East, they foresaw no harvest of
souls. The infidels who inhabited the realm of the Great
Turk were beyond redemption, as apparently were the
pagans who dwelt in India and the far reaches of the
Pacific. Nevertheless, clergymen viewed the East with fascination and wonder and became important influences in
advancing the cause of the Levant and East India companies. Instead of worrying about the souls of the natives,
they professed concern for the spiritual state of Englishmen who carried the first seeds of empire to the Levant and
India.

The trading companies, on their part, were officially
desirous of the ministrations of godly preachers. Very
quickly managing directors learned that the East had

moral hazards for apprentices and merchants alike, and they sought the aid of clergymen in teaching the prudential virtues so prized in bourgeois society. Moreover, like the ship captains who sailed the Spanish seas, they believed that the worship of God was a good insurance—indeed, a profitable investment. For the Lord blessed the worshipful merchant and sent prosperity to voyages which observed godly discipline. Hence, strict rules were drawn up for the conduct of mariners and merchants; ministers were employed at the expense of the trading companies; and good books were provided for the pious edification of the pioneers who laid the foundation of English trade in the East.

The Near East had long been a region of mingled fascination and horror. Since the Crusades, occasional Englishmen had ventured across the Mediterranean and brought back strange tales of the Turks, or the fierce Mohammedans of North Africa, or the wonders of Egypt and the Holy Land.[1] Even after the Reformation, Protestant travelers sometimes made semireligious pilgrimages to Jerusalem and performed their devotions at the Church of the Holy Sepulchre. Invariably travelers dwelt upon the wickedness of the infidels. As Turk and Saracen became a popular theme of poets and dramatists, the public learned to regard the East as a land of colossal iniquity, where men might lose not only their lives but also their immortal souls. For the ill-gotten rewards of piracy on the Barbary Coast, English seamen occasionally cast their lot with the infidels; and sometimes unfortunate captives, to preserve their physical integrity or their lives, "turned Turk." Elizabethans heard with horror many tales of these "renegadoes," and the Church, from time to time, devised prayers supplicating strength for the unfortunates, that they might resist torture and apostasy. Even the merchant who traded under the protection of the Great Turk or the Great Mogul underwent grave risks—more subtle perhaps, but nevertheless disastrous to his spiritual welfare. He might be corrupted by the loose living about him, and he might fall a victim to the temptation of earning easy money at the expense of the company—both violations of the fundamental morals of churchgoing citizens and shareholders. In their zeal for religion and morality, therefore, the official attitude of the governing bodies of the trading companies presents a remarkable demonstration of middle-class ethics.

The concern of the Levant and East India companies over religion did not differ from that of the older established trading companies, except in intensity. The Merchant Adventurers and the Russia Company customarily employed chaplains for their voyages and their stations abroad. Laymen as well as preachers remarked on the religious state of foreign regions and took religion into their calculations in scouting new places for trade. Anthony Jenkinson, for example, in his travels from Moscow to Bokhara, in 1558, for the Russia Company, was distressed at the religious condition of the natives of Astrakan. "At that time," he writes, "it had bene an easie thing to have converted that wicked Nation to the Christian faith, if the Russes themselves had bene good Christians." [2] Traders knew that native religions might vitally affect business relations, and their interest represented a mixture of concern over the practical aspects of the problem and a humanitarian regret that so many misguided pagans were headed for certain perdition.

Almost from its foundation in 1582, the Levant Company included chaplains among its necessary personnel.[3] A chaplain could not be employed until he had preached a trial sermon before the court of the company and satisfied the assembled shareholders as to his orthodoxy, his morality, and his good sense. Preachers were assigned to Aleppo and Constantinople, and, later in the seventeenth century, to Smyrna. The preachers appointed to Constantinople had a dual function as ministers to the company and chaplains to the English ambassador. In a few instances their official sermons were of sufficient interest to warrant publication at home. One of these, *A Sermon Preached At Constantinople, in the Vines of Perah, at the Funerall of . . . Lady Anne Glover . . . By William Forde . . . lately Preacher to the right Honourable Ambassadour, and the rest of the English Nation resident there* (1616), is a conventional obituary, but it commemorates an incident as macabre as any in Elizabethan drama. Grief-stricken over the death of his wife, Sir Thomas Glover, the ambassador, refused to have her buried, but packed her coffin with bran and kept it in his house until the chaplain and others finally persuaded him to bury her. Although the sermon only hints at the ambassador's morbid grief, the news of it reached England in letters, and many readers, therefore, must have viewed the obituary with peculiar interest.[4]

In one of Sir Thomas Smythe's first letters as governor of the Levant Company, written early in 1600 to William Biddulph, chaplain at Aleppo,[5] he suggests the responsibility of the preachers in preserving the morality and good conduct of their English flocks. "You will contyneue and proceade in your charge," the governor directs, "both in the instruccon of our people in knowledge of Religyon and in reproving and rebuking whatsoeuer you shall ether see or be dewly informed of to deserve reproof or admonition." No word is said about proselyting the Mohammedans, for that was strictly forbidden. In no sense were these preachers missionaries. Their business was to see that English apprentices and factors behaved themselves in accordance with the moral and religious code of the company.

The Levantine chaplains, like the preachers who went to other regions, not only served as the official guardians of English morality but, officially and unofficially, became publicity agents. More literate and having more time than their merchant and apprentice colleagues, they wrote long descriptive letters about the strange places and peoples of the Near East. Some of these letters were in the nature of reports to the home office; others were personal communications to friends and relatives. In both cases, however, the messages circulated sufficiently to create renewed interest in the regions described.

The letters of William Biddulph, written from Aleppo, illustrate the process. They became the core of a descriptive narrative, edited and published in 1609 by one Theophilus Lavender as *The Travels Of certaine Englishmen into Africa, Asia,* . . . The chaplain had four companions on his travels: two merchants, a gentleman, and a jeweler, whose letters Lavender also utilized in putting together this account of the Near East, designed to attract the attention of

English Protestants. Mixed with geographical descriptions were observations derogatory to the Catholics, especially the Jesuits, who were ridiculed for their cupidity. A mock hymn in Latin and English suggests that the Jesuits had sometimes proved better traders than the English merchants. One of Biddulph's letters, printed by Purchas, describes a visit to the Holy Land and a prayer service at Aleppo on receipt of the news of the death of Queen Elizabeth and the accession of James I.[6]

From his chaplaincy at Aleppo, Biddulph apparently was translated to India, but as a trader, rather than preacher, of the East India Company. After his appointment as factor at Surat on October 18, 1614, he maintained a fluent correspondence with officials at home.[7]

Publishers realized that the name of a preacher would lend authority to travel narratives; furthermore, a preacher's reputation for truth would take off the curse of mendacity too often attributed to lay travelers. Hence, Thomas Thorpe, in 1611, brought out a book by the Reverend John Cartwright entitled, *The Preachers Travels.* It describes a private journey, begun in 1599, by a young cleric of Oxford, whose adventures took him over land and sea to most of the important regions of the Near East. His account concludes "With the description of a Port in the Persian gulf, commodious for our East Indian Merchants; and a briefe rehearsall of some grosse absu[r]dities in the Turkish Alcoran." On his return to England, Cartwright was appointed a chaplain by the East India Company, but was dismissed for his part in persuading Captain George Weymouth to turn back in 1602 from a search for the Northwest Passage. Cartwright refers to this fiasco in the preface to the reader, whom he implores to "moderate thy opinion of our former proceedings," and adds that "some maleuo-lent tongues haue especially shot out their venemous poy-son against me." Cartwright's narrative, which stops with his arrival in Aleppo, is straightforward and vivid—pre-cisely the sort of document that readers at home found both entertaining and useful. The learning and the reli-gious profession of the writer were taken as a guarantee of its veraciousness by many a reader, who may have doubted the tales of the Sherley brothers, but in Cartwright's story found confirmation of the peculiarities and marvels of the East. Significantly, the second edition of the letters of William Biddulph and his companions, brought out in the year after Cartwright's book appeared, emphasized the chaplain's part by entitling the work, *The Travels of Foure English Men and a Preacher*.[8]

Since factors were usually too busy with commerce to supply elaborate reports on matters not concerned with trade, chaplains became important disseminators of infor-mation about the Levantine world. A part of their official responsibility was to prepare news reports, some of which found their way into print. "These are the newes of Turky," says Charles Robson, the chaplain, in *Newes From Aleppo* (1628); "we should be glad to heare some from England. I haue not had so much as one Letter, but from Master Fethplate (who writeth businesse, not newes)." This appeal by the chaplain for reciprocal news from home was addressed to a friendly vicar in Sussex whom he had known when he was a fellow of Queen's College, Oxford.

Though Robson's letter was a personal message to a friend, it was deemed suitable for printing as a news pamphlet. Most of its pages were devoted to a readable and succinct account of the outward voyage through the Mediterranean, followed by a description of the countries adjacent, with emphasis on the potential fruitfulness of the land around Aleppo, "vnhappy in nothing but the cursed Lords of it, the Turkes." The author, however, is confident that some day the Lord will "restore it to the true owners, the Christians." [9] Meanwhile, it should be the object of Englishmen to establish themselves advantageously.

The traders who made the most use of preachers in the expansion eastward were the fraternity of the East India Company, which was chartered by Queen Elizabeth on December 31, 1600. Our ideas about the morals of the East India Company have been colored by reading the oratory of Burke and his colleagues against Warren Hastings, and we are likely to forget that the first governor, Sir Thomas Smythe, was a man of exemplary piety, who presided like a bishop over the meetings of stockholders and mingled prayers with all financial transactions. In 1617, for example, when the ships "Globe" and "Peppercorn" returned from India with a rich profit for the shareholders, the governor called them to prayers and in his speech reminded them that God would increase their profits in proportion to their gratitude, and "that therefore all ought to lift up their hearts unto God to be thankful for the same, and to be more thankful by reason His blessings have exceeded; not doubting but the more thankful we be, the more His blessings will increase." [10] The profound belief in the profits of godliness permeated the actions of the company and resulted in a vast deal of attention to the choice of preachers and provisions for pious observances in its ships and factories.

The selection of chaplains was no perfunctory duty intrusted to a minor official. The court minutes show that the governor himself made it his business to write to Oxford and Cambridge for recommendations, and that, as in the case of the Levant Company, candidates for appointment were required to preach trial sermons, on prescribed texts, before the officers of the company. These businessmen were connoisseurs of sermons, and they savored the homilies with the skill of professional doctors of divinity. Various qualities determined the fitness of appointees: learning, eloquence, skill in debate, honesty, and willingness to forego the profits of private trade. This last consideration was troublesome, for even preachers were tempted occasionally by the easy profits derived from Indian goods and tried to send home a bale or two of salable articles. The desire of the preachers for a taste of prosperity is understandable, for their usual stipend was £50 per year—sometimes less, rarely more. But company officials impressed upon their young ministers the heavenly virtue of poverty for those who followed the divine calling.

The company endeavored to find chaplains, made of stern stuff, who could resist the temptations of the world, the flesh, and the devil. Many were called to preach before Sir Thomas and his colleagues, but few were chosen after the officers had appraised their sermons and examined their private lives. The case of a Mr. Sturdivant, who applied for appointment in March, 1609, illustrates the care exercised in choosing preachers. Bearing strong recommendations, he was summoned to preach before the governor and a committee, from the text, "Blessed be the poor in spirit." Although his sermon apparently was satisfactory, an investigation of his private life showed "that he hath a straggling humour, can frame himself to all company, as he finds men affected, and delighteth in tobacco and wine," whereupon the committee reported that "he is conceived unfit for one of his profession, and for the Company's employment." [11] During the early years of the company's history, scores of preachers appeared before Sir Thomas Smythe and his committees and underwent searching examinations. If the company was not always happy in its choices, the fault was not a result of failure to look closely into the abilities, lives, and characters of the candidates. Occasionally a minister of unusual versatility was discovered, as in the case of a certain "William Evans, a preacher at Barking, who has been in Spain and the West Indies, practised physic for 20 years in France and England, and studied divinity eight years." Mr. Evans was readily employed in March, 1614, and, since he combined the skill of preacher and surgeon, his stipend was increased to £60.[12]

The ability to confound Catholic controversialists in debate was a desirable quality in an East India chaplain, and much prized by resident factors, who found themselves in competition with Jesuit missionaries. Joseph Salbank, a factor at Agra, wrote to the company on November 22, 1617, pleading for a good controversialist as well as a devout pastor. "Pray, censure it not as a part of boldness in me to advertise you of one matter [which] may seem much fitter to be spoken or written by another man than myself, even of your preachers and ministers [that] you send hither to reside amongst us, and to break unto us the blessed manna of the heavenly doctrine," Salbank remarks. "Very convenient it will be for you to provide such as are not only sufficient and solid divines, that may be able to encounter with the arch enemies of our religion (if occasion should so require), those main supporters of the hierarchy of the church of Rome—I mean the Jesuits, or rather (as I may truly term them) Jebusites, whereof some are mingled here amongst us in several places of this King's dominion —but also godly, zealous and devout persons, such as may with their piety and purity of life give good example to those with whom they live, whereby they will no less instruct and feed their little flock committed unto them by the sincerity of the doctrine which they teach them." [13] Appointments were sometimes influenced by the hope that the candidate selected would prove a mighty antagonist of popish enemies. For instance, on October 26, 1614, the Reverend William Leske was employed at more than double the usual stipend, "the Company being well satisfied of his learning and gravity, and being able to contest with and hold argument with the Jesuits, who are busy at Surat." [14] Though Mr. Leske most certainly proved an argumentative preacher, he fell short of the gravity and godly zeal prescribed by Salbank.

The East India Company did not feel that its official duty was done when it selected a competent preacher and sent him forth to labor in the vineyards of Surat or Agra, or to minister to the sailors who manned its great merchant ships. Strict rules of conduct were imposed, and provisions were made for religious observances on land and sea. The religious exercises on board the East India ships followed a pattern prescribed for many earlier Elizabethan voyages, but from company officials they received a consistent supervision which was remarkable even in that age of piety. From the governor down to individual ship captains, there was a united effort to see that regular prayer services were observed and proper sermons preached during voyages. On the rare occasions when a ship's commander failed in his religious responsibilities, he was the subject of complaints, not only from the chaplains but from the seamen themselves. If we cannot imagine East Indiamen as seagoing conventicles, we have certain knowledge of their strict adherence to a schedule of prayers that would have done credit to a missionary community.

Chaplains and ship commanders were afraid that neglect of the prescribed religious duties might lead to investigation and possible rebuke or dismissal. That accusations of such neglect were seriously regarded by company officials is clear from evidence in the court minutes. In February, 1619, the Reverend James Rynd found himself in difficulties because Barnard Wright, purser's mate of the ship "Moon," asserted that "prayers were never read in that ship but when there was nothing else to do." Rynd replied that this was a gross untruth, and that he had "read prayers with some portion of the Scripture twice a day, except during his sickness, when Sir Thomas Dale did so." [15] Captain Nicholas Downton, commander of the fleet which sailed from England in March, 1613, was the object of bitter complaints by the Reverend Peter Rogers, who charged that he ridiculed East India Company officials for arrogating to themselves virtues which they did not possess, and said that, though not a few of them professed religion, "he always found those that made not so great a show to be more generous, more bountiful, and the like." Furthermore, Rogers alleged, the commander neglected prayers on week days and often failed to attend religious service on Sunday, "to the great offence and discouragement of many." [16] Although Downton was a successful officer, whose fleet won a great victory over the Portuguese, Rogers' complaints resulted in a solemn investigation. Thomas Kerridge, one of the most religious as well as responsible factors in India, wrote from Ajmere to Sir Thomas Smythe, on March 26, 1615, hinting that Rogers was the tool of a faction hostile to Downton and might better have been a peacemaker. Moreover, Kerridge adds, Rogers was a disappointment and had not proved useful in a place which required "profound learning to defend God's cause against these cunning Jesuits." [17] Downton's death in Bantam on August 6, 1615, saved him from having to answer the complaints in person. If a leader as capable and useful as Captain Downton could be held accountable for failure to attend prayers and sermons, we can be certain that the requirements were rarely relaxed for subordinates.

The journals and logs of the voyages give abundant evidence of the rules and the religious observances customary at sea. For example, the journal kept by Ralph Crosse, purser of the ship "Hoseander" in the Tenth Voyage, of

1612, begins with the orders issued by the fleet commander, Captain Thomas Best, for compulsory attendance at divine service, morning and evening, on each of the ships, when prayers and the Scriptures were read, "in all soberness, as in the presence of God." No man was permitted to be absent, either willingly or negligently, on pain of punishment. Swearing and blaspheming were strictly forbidden. Punishment for the first oath was three blows from the bole of the master's whistle, with three additional blows for each oath up to four. After that, the culprit had to stand in the bilboes for twenty-four hours without food and drink. Likewise, card and dice play, drunkenness, malice, envy, backbiting, slander, and hatred were banned in the interest of "mutuall love and concorde." [18] There was nothing perfunctory in the way these orders were carried out. When Captain Best's fleet encountered a Portuguese flotilla off Surat, the commander himself came aboard the "Hoseander" and delivered a sermon based on texts taken from the Sixteenth Psalm, some of which the purser thought proper to copy in his journal. To the seamen awaiting battle, Captain Best held out a hope of heaven, if death should be their fate, and exhorted them to remember that they could not die for a better country than England. At the end of his pious oration, he drank a cup of wine to the master and the ship's company, "and desired God to give us His blessinge, and so retourned abord his owne shipp to sermon." A further prayer service was held on board the "Hoseander" by Paul Canning, a factor at Surat, and the ship was then made ready for battle.[19] On the Sunday following the successful outcome of the fight, the ships' companies again attended sermons, as was customary on the Sabbath in typical expeditions sent out by the East India Company. When a chaplain was available, he ordinarily made the rounds of the ships in the fleet, but if bad weather prevented such pastoral visitations the master or some merchant aboard held the services and read prayers and sermons.

The East India Company saw to it that ships were amply provided with edifying reading matter. The essentials were a Bible and a Book of Common Prayer, John Foxe's *Book of Martyrs*, and frequently the works of the famous Cambridge divine, William Perkins. For secular reading, Richard Hakluyt's *Voyages* was included. In a commission to John Saris and Gabriel Towerson, for the Eighth Voyage, in 1611, the company provided the writings of Foxe, Hakluyt, and Perkins, and enjoined the factors to read good books and observe the Sabbath. The tradition of pious reading by merchants in India apparently persisted, for in 1666 a group of factors requested a long list of the works of the church fathers, desired for their library.[20] Richard Cocks, an English factor in Japan, noted in his journal for March 9, 1616, that he had lent from his library St. Augustine's *City of God*, "the Turkish History and a book of forme of debitor and creditor"[21]—a mixture of the pious and the practical that was characteristic of the little collections of books taken out by merchants. The East India Company was likewise careful to suppress evil writings. For instance, Captain John Saris was charged on December 16, 1614, with bringing home, or permitting to be brought home in his ship, "certain lascivious books and

pictures," to the "great scandal" of the company, whereupon the governor promised to have them burned or else
"free his house of them and the captain both." [22] If seamen
and factors turned sinners, it was not for lack of official
oversight of their morals.

Although the chaplains had to be orthodox Anglicans in
good standing to pass Sir Thomas Smythe and his committees, the official point of view concerning morals and the
actual behavior of the majority of the company agents was
extremely puritanical, and their very language smacks of
the canting vocabulary ridiculed by Ben Jonson and other
satirists. It was conventional for their business letters to
begin with some pious invocation like "Jesus," or "Eman-
uel," or "Laus Deo," and to end with a dedication to God.
Typical was the tone of a letter from the factors at Surat
reporting the theft of some bars of lead, taken possibly
while they were at prayers. Mingled with prosaic business
details are religious allusions, and the communication closes
with a benediction, "And thus with our prayers for the
preservation of your Worships' healths and prosperous
success to all your worthy designs, we humbly take leave
and commend you to the Almighty's merciful guidance." [23]
Although such formulas were common enough in the early
seventeenth century, the correspondence of the East India
Company is noteworthy for evidences of a belief that God
was a silent, though decisive, partner in their undertakings.
Undoubtedly the piety of the factors in authority sometimes irked less godly Englishmen, who found difficulty
in tolerating an atmosphere of persistent sanctimony.
George Pley, an agent writing from Isfahan on May 15,

1617, to Thomas Kerridge, head of the factors at Surat, unburdens his soul over the abuse heaped upon him by a certain Barker, whom he had rebuked for allegedly dishonest practices in selling ginger; but "it pleased the gentleman to style me with the name of knave, puritan knave, and prying knave, and threadbare knave, menacing that if I had been to stay, he would have dealt with me in another fashion. But alas! in the one I come far short of my duty towards God (yet wish I could be more zealous for God's glory), and so in that kind deserve not the name of a Puritan." [24]

An example of godliness was set by Sir Thomas Roe, sent out in 1616, at the behest of the East India Company, as royal ambassador to the court of the Great Mogul. Sir Thomas would not stir without a preacher in his train. When his chaplain died, he sadly observed that "thus it pleased God to lay a great affliction on mee and my famely for our sinnes," and wrote posthaste to Surat for another preacher, for he could not "liue the life of an Atheist." [25] The chaplain sent was Edward Terry, whose account of Roe's mission gives the writer a permanent place in the annals of eastward expansion. Since Roe's duties at the court at Agra included circumvention of the Jesuits who were believed to be plotting against the English merchants,[26] he needed all the ecclesiastical help he could get. Combined with his piety, Roe had a fund of common sense which helped to increase his influence with the English traders in India. His letters were filled with shrewd advice and pious admonitions; yet he never let religion run away with his sound business judgment. On one occa-

sion, for instance, he reproves the factors at Surat for
putting in charge of certain business affairs a preacher who
was "too gentle to govern," who "lost money by the account," and "gave away many things in presents." [27] Religion with Roe was a necessary concomitant of living and a
guide to worldly success. Along with godliness, he urged
frugality. "You shall live frugally, soberly, like merchants,
without prodigal expenses, the country being cheap, and
travel with as few servants as may stand with safety," he
instructs traders going into Persia. [28] Constantly he was ex-
horting his countrymen to observe the religious and moral
code which was the cornerstone of English commercial
society, and characteristically he closed his letters of advice
with some such devout wish as "God bless all your endeavours and send us all the fruition of His kingdom." [29]

The piety of the Englishmen who were the spearhead
of commercial expansion to the east in the early seventeenth century was an asset worth maintaining by all the
powers of persuasion and authority that the East India
Company and the government could muster. Since communication was slow and difficult, company factors, and
even subordinate agents, had to be intrusted with far more
responsibility than would be necessary today. Peculiarly
important, therefore, was a strict regard for the prudential
virtues of frugality, sobriety, diligence, and honesty. Hence
these virtues received especial emphasis in religious teach-
ings. It was the pious hope and dream of Sir Thomas
Smythe and his colleagues that in every voyage God would
go along as a sort of spiritual supercargo, and that, in the
factories abroad, He would preside as a censor of morals

and auditor invisible. Evidences of religion on the part of employees was pleasing to the officials back home, and they could all sincerely appreciate the sentiments of Ralph Preston, a factor at Surat, who wrote in a business letter, dated January 1, 1615, that he would "ever praise God for you and never cease to pray for your healths and prosperities with increase of commerce and the end everlasting life, which God grant for his son Christ's sake." [30] A servant like Preston, Sir Thomas felt, would observe the rules of the company and induce Providence to reward his endeavors.

The wisdom of the company's religious policies was demonstrated in the high standard of conduct maintained by its employees and the profits which their diligent application to business brought to the shareholders. Verily God smiled upon them, and they were usually able to circumvent, not only the hostile Jesuits, but also, on occasion, the shrewd Protestants of the Dutch East India Company, whose chaplains and businessmen subscribed to a similar code of bourgeois morals.[31] The English merchants in India made it their business to uphold the good reputation of their country. Because free-lance Englishmen were not subject to the strict controls exercised over company workers, the factors at Surat urged that no gentlemen-travelers or other unattached persons be permitted to come to India. Such Englishmen, their report points out, become disorderly and idle, observing neither Christian services nor native customs, and thus bring the whole English nation into disrepute.[32]

Since the East India Company, like other trading companies of the seventeenth century, also desired to maintain a good name before the public at home, it found the preachers in its employ useful in spreading a favorable report. Sir Thomas Smythe even directed certain charities toward that end. On October 10, 1614, the company court voted to relieve the poverty of "some poor preachers in this town, to have their prayers for the good and prosperity of the Company's voyages" [33]—an action that won the approval of the clergy but brought a great clamor of poor preachers seeking the company's benevolence. Influential clergymen were sometimes given official recognition—and incidental financial rewards—in the hope of gaining their good will. Among such ministers were John Preston, the famous Puritan divine of Cambridge, Theophilus Field, the King's chaplain, and Dr. Thomas James, librarian of the Bodleian, who, in 1617 and 1618, were sworn gratis to be free brethren of the company.[34] Among the regular shareholders in the various joint-stock voyages were many members of the clergy,[35] who must have taken considerable comfort in the great official concern over religion. With profits accruing from successful investments, they would have found it hard to criticize so worthy an enterprise.

Some of the clergy demonstrated their good will by publishing sermons or other treatises favorable or useful to the company. Like modern corporations, the East India merchants were very sensitive to criticism and sought to counteract hostile comment with friendly publicity. For this purpose, Dr. Samuel Page of Deptford was called in at a critical moment, on March 29, 1616, to preach a thanksgiving sermon before the governor and members of the company, in celebration of the fleet's safe return. Governor Smythe and his colleagues had particular reasons for wanting to make much of the occasion. During the previous year, one Robert Kayll (or Keale), an ardent isolationist, in a shrewdly designed pamphlet entitled *The Trades Increase*, had brought to notice recent wrecks of East India ships and had bitterly attacked the company's policies of expansion. Sir Dudley Digges replied officially with *The Defence of Trade* (1615), which stressed the value and profits to the commonwealth of East Indian commerce and enumerated the benevolences of the corporation, particularly the money spent to relieve "poore painfull Preachers of the Gospell." [36] But so distressed was Smythe over Kayll's blasphemy against business that he sought the aid of the Archbishop of Canterbury, who promised to suppress the hostile book if Smythe desired, but advised instead "that it should rather be suffered to die than be suppressed, which would cause many men to seek after it the more earnestly." Although Smythe's attorneys reported that *The Trades Increase* contained some points "very near to treason and all the rest very dangerous," [37] the company decided not to insist upon outright suppression. No opportunity, however, was neglected thereafter to reply to issues raised in the controversy. For that reason, the completion of a profitable voyage by the East India fleet, early in the spring of 1616, provided a desirable theme for Samuel Page's sermon, published a month after its delivery, under the title of *God be thanked*. Appended to the sermon was

77

a little prayer book, the *Diuine Sea-seruice,* supplying prayers for the sixteen most urgent occasions in a seaman's experience.

The religious sentiments expressed by Dr. Page might have been written by Sir Thomas Smythe himself, so perfectly did they mirror the official point of view. The minister emphasized particularly the godliness of commerce with the Indies—a trade useful alike to the adventurers and to the commonwealth. "Wee reioyce," Page declares, "we the people of this Congregation, who in our publique meetings in this house of Prayer, haue euer ioyned in common supplications before the Throne of Grace, for the good successe of your voyages, and for the preseruation of those persons and goods which you aduenture vpon the great waters." [38] Although some investors and seamen may have suffered woe in the voyages, Page asserts that most complaints have been unjust—the result of human frailty, impatience, and "clamorousnesse." Furthermore, the blame for recent shipwrecks attaches to the whole people of England, and to the investors no less than to the seafarers in the voyages, because God had looked down and observed their sinfulness. To prevent future disaster, he fervently pleads that everyone concerned with the welfare of the nation and its commerce repent of his sins and pray diligently to the Almighty. Then, and then only, will prosperity be unbroken. To the traders and sailors who go abroad he issues a warning against the danger of absorbing foreign iniquities. When all observe the commandments of God, they can expect to return home, as in the present voyage, like Joseph's brethren, "euery mans sack filled with the good corne of the Land of Egypt, and euery mans mony in his sackes mouth." [39] Page's sermon was both an affirmation of the religious policies of the East India Company and a plea for more widespread observance of its tenets. Printing the sermon was a further step toward stopping the mouths of critics who had spread the heresies set forth in *The Trades Increase.*

Not all the writings of the East India preachers were so obviously propagandic in design as Dr. Page's *God be thanked,* but other publications by clergymen served a useful purpose. Dr. John Wood, for example, besides preaching aboard the company's ships, became so proficient in the science of navigation that in 1618 he brought out a treatise on the subject, entitled *The True Honor of Navigation and Navigators.* Grateful officials commended the work and presented the author with a purse of twenty jacobuses. [40] Henry Lord, appointed a chaplain in 1624, printed *A Display of two forraigne sects in the East Indies . . . the Banians . . . And . . . the Persees* (1630) to supplement, from first-hand observation, material concerning these pagans which the Reverend Samuel Purchas—also a great favorer of the East India Company—had included in his vast collection of travel narratives. Not only does the East India Company import useful commodities, Lord points out in a dedication to the governor and adventurers, but it also performs another valuable service by acquainting "the home-residers with the manners and Customes of the People in transmarine Kingdoms of the world." The agents for this information service were diligent clerics like Lord and Samuel Purchas.

Another treatise which carried the news of the East India Company's activities to the ear of the royal court was prepared by a man already mentioned, Edward Terry, Sir Thomas Roe's chaplain, and presented to Prince Charles on the preacher's return to England in 1622. Although Purchas included in his collection a version of Terry's travels, the complete account did not receive separate publication until 1655, when it appeared with fresh moralizations by the author.

Behind the publication of one sermon, which flattered Sir Thomas Smythe and the adventurers of the East India Company, lay such a bizarre story of a chaplain's moral collapse as might have provided Somerset Maugham with a counterpart for the plot of *Rain*. The preacher was William Leske. Because of his reputed learning, Sir Thomas Roe had requested his services as chaplain, but Edward Terry had been sent instead. Meanwhile, Leske began his pastorate at Surat, where the temptations of the flesh proved too strong and he disgraced his flock by taking to drink and frequenting brothels. An occasional preacher had hitherto proved incompetent, but no scandal like this had previously befallen the English community, not even among the lay brethren. So shocked and horrified were pious Thomas Kerridge and his colleagues that they quickly brought charges against the erring minister and implored Captain Henry Pepwell, commander of the fleet, forthwith to remove him from their midst. Not only had Leske been drunk in bawdy-houses, but he had paid the prostitutes with counterfeit coins, to the further shame of the merchants, and had threatened the life of Kerridge.[41] Thus it was that in the summer of 1617 the chaplain was shipped home on board the "Globe." During the voyage he continued to exercise his office and on arrival printed *A Sermon Preached Aboard of the Globe the 18. of May, Anno 1617. At an Anchor by the Cape of Good Hope.* The printed sermon was designed to please the company officials, whom it praised for their wisdom and benefactions. At the same time, in a letter, Leske claimed that he was the victim of a conspiracy by the factors, who resented his reproof of their own sins. Given a hearing before a committee, he was found guilty as charged, but the company hushed up the affair, and even allowed him to dispose of two bales of goods which he had brought home. But Leske's behavior stands in notable contrast to the usual conduct of East India laymen and ministers. The eagerness of the company officials to keep such scandalous news from being noised abroad indicates their concern over the reputation of their servants for moral probity and religious devotion.

Many of the preachers who served in the Far East were men of ability and some distinction. Nor were they invariably subservient to the officials of the company. Patrick Copland, for instance, one of the ablest of the chaplains, was bold to rebuke injustice, often taking the part of the sailors and poor men. A witness testified in 1621 that he "often reproved the commanders in his sermons." [42] That may explain why, on October 10, 1621, he had to answer charges of "disanimating the mariners" in a sermon preceding a fight with the Dutch. Copland had been bold to say that justice was not all on one side, and had pleaded for mutual understanding.[43]

Copland's sermon on the problems involved in Anglo-Dutch rivalry was ill-timed—the hours before battle are not the proper occasion for discussing with sailors and soldiers the pros and cons of their cause—and the official concern over the influence of his remarks focuses attention on an important function of the chaplains. In the language of today, they were morale officers. The preachers had the important responsibility of seeing that Englishmen in the East did not forget the manners and morals of the home land. They constantly reminded the servants of the East India Company of their loyalty to their employer, their country, and their God.

The success of Englishmen in penetrating the East in the first quarter of the seventeenth century owes much to the quality of their beliefs, economic, moral, and religious. If we interpret the East India Company, in terms of our own age, as a corporation of greedy materialists, using religion as a cloak for the exploitation of its own workers and of other people, we show a total misunderstanding of the period. The commercial pioneers of this era possessed a curious idealism which identified economic prosperity and spiritual welfare. The moral code to which they subscribed emphasized material success as an incidental reward for proper conduct; and prosperity, in many a man's thinking, became the barometer of godliness. Commerce and religion went hand in hand, and in the struggle for commercial supremacy in the East merchants and mariners sincerely believed that they were the instruments of Providence. The East India Company individually and collectively reflected the prevailing religious and moral ideas of the commercial classes and made use of these beliefs in developing a great empire east of Suez, where, in the seventeenth century, the best was decidedly not like the worst.

CHAPTER FOUR

A Western Canaan
Reserved for England

DURING the long years of Elizabeth's reign, momentum for expansion into the western world had increased, and envy of Catholic Spain had intensified as Protestant Englishmen realized that they had slept over an opportunity to gain an empire overseas. In the later years of the sixteenth century, a faction of imperialists who discerned the full implications of colonization struggled to arouse public opinion and to counteract the insular policies of more conservative leaders. Gradually England came to see that its destiny as a power depended upon claiming a share of the New World. By the time James I ascended the throne, mercantile groups throughout England and leaders from the nobility, like the Earl of Southampton and the Earl of Warwick, were keenly aware that both profits and national prestige would be the reward of a bold endeavor to settle Englishmen in the Western Hemisphere. Behind this movement was a solid bloc of the more intense Protestants. They resented the Spanish claim to the

New World based on Pope Alexander VI's donation—a claim which had long been a source of bitter remonstrance from both English and Dutch Protestants, who refused to recognize any Pope's authority to exclude them from their natural rights to colonize where they would or could.

The publication in 1583 of an English version of Bartolomé de las Casas' *The Spanish Colonie*, describing "Spanish cruelties and tyrannies, perpetrated in the West Indies," added fuel to the flames of hatred and jealousy of the Spaniards. English controversialists found in the revelations of this Dominican bishop proof of their contention that common humanity required them to rescue the heathen Indians from the atrocities of such wicked oppressors. Few opponents of Spanish aggression failed to quote Las Casas against his countrymen, and Protestant preachers made particular use of his tractate in arousing their congregations against the power of anti-Christ in the New World.

Throughout the first quarter of the seventeenth century, the clergy carried on a vigorous propaganda against Spain and in behalf of western colonization. The main arguments had already been set forth by Richard Hakluyt, who continued his own activity and induced other clergymen to join battle in the cause. One result of this consistent propaganda was the crystallization of a belief that God had especially reserved portions of the western world for the English. In numerous writers and in various ways appears the doctrine that particular regions had been set aside until such time as Englishmen might need to emigrate. Not always were preachers in agreement about the locality of these divinely appointed reservations, for sometimes the land lay in the swamps of Guiana, sometimes in the coral-girt islands of the West Indies, and sometimes on the continent of North America; but always clergymen could find reasons to prove the Almighty's singular care for the prosperity of English colonists who might settle in one of these regions. This idea, ever congenial to national vanity, quickly percolated into the public consciousness and appears in the utterances of preachers and laymen alike. It helped to create an English version of the belief in Manifest Destiny which profoundly influenced colonial enterprise in the seventeenth century.

The clergy were almost unanimous in supporting colonization in America. Both Anglicans and Puritans were equally insistent that England must claim her share of the New World. Several motives prompted them. One was a perfectly sincere belief that God had commanded them to save the souls of the heathen. Actual contact with the Indians somewhat altered these views, and a few of the Puritan clergy later asserted that the Indians were children of the devil who might profitably be wiped out and their lands appropriated. But the prevailing belief was that missionaries must carry the gospel to the savages. An even stronger motive was the desire to checkmate Spain's conversion of the infidels and the establishment of a Catholic empire. A third motive was a widespread notion that the economic salvation of England urgently required relief from overpopulation. Since the clergy in this period were among the most alert of what we would call "social thinkers," they felt it incumbent upon them to discuss that economic problem. A fourth reason for the clergy's interest in America was simply the romantic stimulation that their imaginations had received from reports of the wonders of the new land. As literate men of a sedentary profession, they consumed avidly the narratives of adventure written by travelers and explorers, and reinterpreted these narratives for fresh audiences. And lastly, the new science had found some of its most enthusiastic supporters among men in holy orders. Anglicans and Puritans showed a similar zeal for the science of geography and both were diligent in contributing their scientific knowledge to the advancement of exploration and colonization.

The stock companies, organized to make settlements in the New World, realized the value of the clergy's influence in the promotion of their enterprises and took steps to win the enthusiastic support of the preachers. Noteworthy in this endeavor was the Virginia Company of London, which, from its inception, made a consistent and systematic effort to utilize the clergy to produce a favorable public opinion. From all the evidence now available, it appears that the Virginia Company achieved a remarkable success in gaining and keeping the aid of an able group of pulpit propagandists.

From its foundation in 1606 until its dissolution in 1624, the Virginia Company employed preachers to deliver sermons before the shareholders on stated occasions. It printed these sermons at the expense of the company and distributed them widely. It also rewarded the preachers with payments in cash, and, in some instances, by giving them stock in the company. Dr. John Donne, dean of St. Paul's, was the most distinguished cleric in its pay, but there were many others almost as well known in their time. Moreover, among the shareholders themselves were many clergymen, some of them high in the church, who looked upon the Virginia Company as an enterprise especially ordained to carry out the divine plan. As a result, English pulpits rang with praise of the infant colony on the banks of the James.

The beliefs of that singularly active businessman, Sir Thomas Smythe, first treasurer of the company, may account for the close coöperation between promoters and preachers in the early years of development. Sir Thomas was sincerely pious and his prestige with the clergy was high. In the management of the East India Company he had already demonstrated his concern for religion and had tested to his own satisfaction the value of preachers in such an enterprise. No preacher was more profoundly convinced than he that his endeavors would prosper if he zealously promoted the Lord's work. The projected colony in Virginia offered a greater religious opportunity than the Far East, where the necessity of avoiding offense to Mohammedan and Hindoo potentates curbed missionary zeal. Smythe therefore encouraged plans to convert the Indians and quickly made his Virginia undertaking the darling of the clergy. A part of their enthusiasm can be traced to the deliberate policies of the treasurer.

We should not jump to the conclusion, however, that Smythe's primary objectives were charitable and philanthropic, or that he was motivated by unselfish missionary zeal. Private profits were his chief desire, as, indeed, they were the main concern of Smythe's successor, Sir Edwin

Sandys, who likewise was a deeply religious man, greatly interested in the spiritual welfare of the colonists and the heathen.[1] Smythe and Sandys might quarrel over details of policy, but they were united in the belief that religion offered one of the best insurances of success. During the administration of the Smythe group to 1619, and of the Sandys group from 1619 to 1624, preachers received marked favors from the company and proved staunch supporters of the undertaking.

The year 1609 was critical in the affairs of the company. News from the struggling little settlement at Jamestown was bad; the colonists had fared ill during the previous year and stories of their tribulations got around. The investors in the stock saw little hope of riches and began to grumble. Worse still, rumors were afloat that King James, fearful of offending Spain, was about to force the abandonment of the enterprise. At this juncture, new letters patent were issued which shifted responsibility for the rule of the colony from direct royal authority to the council of the company.[2] Immediately the company started a vigorous campaign to arouse public interest in Virginia, and pamphleteers and preachers vied with each other in their commendation of a project that urgently needed further stock subscriptions.

Historians and bibliographers have often discussed the subsequent ballads, books, and pamphlets that described the glories of Virginia, but the full significance of the sermons on the subject has been overlooked.[3] These sermons provide one of the best illustrations in the period of the essential harmony between religion and business enterprise.

Eager as were the ministers to commend English expansion into the New World, the burst of pulpit oratory in 1609 in praise of Virginia was not all spontaneous. Sir Thomas Smythe and his fellow officers were directly responsible. They chose certain popular ministers to preach before the shareholders and then printed their sermons as quickly as possible so that they might reach a wider audience.

The choice for the first official sermon fell upon William Symonds, preacher at Saint Savior's, Southwark, and a former fellow of Magdalen College, Oxford, who had confuted the papists and had achieved a reputation for deep learning by the publication of *Pisgah Evangelica* (1605), a commentary on the Book of Revelation. Symonds had also played with the idea of going to Virginia—an ambition later realized and revealed in observations which he wrote for Captain John Smith's *Generall Historie Of Virginia* (1624). On the morning of April 25, 1609, he rose to address the men who had invested their funds, their energy, and their hopes in a colony in America—men whom the preacher described as the "Advancers Of The Standart of Christ, among the Gentiles, the Aduenturers for the Plantation of Virginia." [4] Appropriately, he chose as his text God's promise to Abraham, from Genesis 12:1-3: "For the Lord had said vnto Abram, Get thee out of thy Countrey, and from thy kindred, and from thy fathers house, vnto the land that I will shew thee. And I will make of thee a great nation, and will blesse thee, and make thy name great, and thou shalt be a blessing. I will blesse them also that blesse thee, and curse them that curse thee, and in thee shall all the families of the earth be blessed." By a casuistry easy for a theologian, particularly one who had recently interpreted the prophecies of Revelation, Symonds transferred this promise from Abraham to the English. Thus formally he gave currency to a belief which by iteration soon became a cardinal point of doctrine among preachers and laymen alike—that the English were divinely appointed as another chosen people to establish themselves in the promised lands of the New World.

To objections against colonizing that were raised by isolationists Symonds has answers backed by scriptural authority. The right of conquest had troubled some men of conscience, but Symonds points out that Christians are commanded to carry the message of Christ to the heathen, and, "if these obiecters had any braines in their head, but those which are sicke, they could easily finde a difference betweene a bloudy inuasion, and the planting of a peaceable Colony, in a waste country, where the people doe liue but like Deere in heards." Such objections, he thinks, are "hatched of some popish egge." [5] Indeed, Symonds, like many preachers who followed him, maintains that the Catholics are a sinister and dangerous enemy of English colonies in the New World and of Virginia in particular. He thinks the English clergy are partly to blame for Catholic success, because they have listened to unprofitable questions at home instead of saving souls abroad. "It is a shame," he laments, "that the Iesuites and Friers, that accompany euery ship, should be so diligent to destroy souls, and wee not seeke the tender lambes." Then addressing the adventurers, Symonds urges them not to be discouraged over what he describes as "the snorting idleness of the ministry," but to go on courageously, confident of the blessing of God.[6] Within less than two weeks after delivery, Symonds' sermon was licensed for printing [7] and appeared under the title of *Virginia. A Sermon Preached At White-Chappel, In The Presence of . . . the Aduenturers and Planters of Virginia, . . . Published For The Benefit And Vse Of The Colony, Planted, And to bee Planted there, and for the Aduancement of their Christian Purpose.*

Three days after Symonds' appearance before the shareholders, another London preacher, Robert Gray, sometime scholar of St. John's College, Cambridge, and rector of St. Benet Sherehog, dated a sermon from his house in Sithes Lane and published it as *A Good Speed to Virginia.* It may have appeared on the bookstalls even ahead of Symonds', for on May 3 it was licensed for printing. Dedicated to the adventurers of the Virginia Company, it too was an official publication and presented an elaborate justification of the Virginia enterprise. The reasons advanced served as a complement to Symonds' arguments. The passage from Joshua 17:14–18 which Gray chose as text is significant of the development of ideas about England's right to territory in the New World. A portion of that text, as quoted by Gray, reads: "Then the children of Ioseph spake vnto Ioshua, saying, why hast thou giue me but one lot, and one portion to inherite, seeing I am a great people? Ioshua then answered, if thou beest much people, get thee vp to the wood, and cut trees for thy selfe in the land of the Perizzites, & of the Giants, if mount Ephraim be too narrow for thee." The text concludes with the promise, "Therefore the

Mountain shal be thine, for it is a wood, and thou shalt cut it downe, and the endes of it shall be thine, & thou shalt cast out the Canaanites thogh they haue Iron Charets, and though they be strong."

With scriptural quotations to support his assertions, Gray proves that Englishmen have a solemn duty to seek out fresh lands to relieve the congestion at home. If these foreign countries are inhabited by savages, then, as the Israelites cast out the Canaanites, so Englishmen must take the land from the idolatrous heathen. But Gray suggests that it would be better if they could first convert the heathen and then peaceably move into the country. The sword is the last resort. Although the children of Joseph had an express command to destroy idolaters, Gray thinks "we must first trie all means before weapons, and when we take them into our hands, necessitie of preseruing our owne liues must rather moue vs to destroy the enemyes of God, then either ambition, or greedinesse of gaine, or crueltie, or anie priuate respect whatsoeuer." [8] But the land of the heathen must be claimed at any cost for the children of God, who will repay the idolaters by bringing them the gospel message and reducing them to civil society. To us this sounds cynical and cold-blooded. But to the seventeenth-century preacher it was logical and just, and there is no reason to question Gray's religious devotion and pious sincerity. Since Adam's sin, God had made distinctions between peoples and it was proper for godly Englishmen to take the lands of sinful worshipers of the devil.

Gray heaps scorn upon shortsighted folk who object to colonization because they see no hope of immediate profit.

Such people are fainthearted and brutish. Men must plant and build, not for themselves alone but for posterity. In the text of his sermon he repeats a common Renaissance theme that he had emphasized in his dedication: the fame and immortality certain to be the reward of adventurers who have a care for the renown of His Majesty, the good of their country, and the advancement of God's glory. Gray rebukes croaking grumblers who complain that failure is inevitable because Raleigh's earlier schemes collapsed, and he shrewdly refers such doubting Thomases to an answer in another official piece of company publicity, *Nova Britannia. Offring Most Excellent fruites by Planting in Virginia. Exciting all such as be well affected to further the same* (1609).[9] This tract, presumably written by Alderman Robert Johnson, one of the promoters of the company, is itself as pious as a sermon and stresses the great expenses already incurred in carrying the gospel to the Indians, whom God had reserved until this last age to be saved by the English. *Nova Britannia* also warns against the danger and deceit of papists and seminary priests.

On May 28, one month after Gray finished his tract, Daniel Price, chaplain to Prince Henry, used the pulpit at Paul's Cross to rebuke the critics of Virginia and praise the undertaking. His defense, published as *Sauls Prohibition Staide . . . with a reproofe of those that traduce the Honourable Plantation of Virginia. Preached in a Sermon Commaunded at Pauls Crosse* (1609), was dedicated to the Lord Chancellor. As the utterance of a fashionable London preacher, it carried particular weight. Price had also gained special merit in the eyes of businessmen by the publication

94

of *The Marchant* (1608), a sermon preached at Paul's Cross, in which he glorified the commercial groups of the city. In *Sauls Prohibition Staide* he paints a fearful picture of the imminent punishment of the city's liars in the fires of hell. After describing the special punishments reserved for the libelers of Virginia, he interpolates a passage praising in terms of a real-estate promoter the riches to be found in the colony. "The Philosopher [i.e., the scientist] commendeth the Temperature," Price declares; "the Marchant the commodity, the Politician the oportunity, the Diuine, the Pietie, in conuerting so many thousand soules. The Virginian desireth it, and the Spaniard enuyeth vs, and yet our lasie, drousie, yet barking Countrimen traduce it, who should honour it, if it were but for the remembrance of that Virgine Queen of eternal memory, who was first godmother to that land and Nation. As also that Virgine Country may in time proue to vs the Barne of Britaine, as Sicily was to Rome, or the Garden of the world as was Thessaly, or the Argosie of the world as is Germany." [10] To timid investors the preacher brings an optimistic message of cheer. Tangible profits may be expected soon, and to these will be added immense future benefits, in this world and the next. Each individual who has a hand in the business will receive "an vnspeakeable blessing." By converting the heathen, Price assures his audience, "you will make . . . A Sauadge country to become a sanctifyed Country; you will obtaine their best commodities; they will obtaine the sauing of their Soules; you will enlarge the boundes of this Kingdome, nay the bounds of heauen." [11]

During the spring of 1609 several preachers not directly connected with the Virginia Company lent the weight of their influence to the schemes for colonization. Most prominent of these was Richard Crakanthorpe, chaplain to Dr. Thomas Ravis, Bishop of London. Crakanthorpe had gained a reputation at Queen's College, Oxford, for his learning, and at the beginning of James's reign had gone as chaplain of the English embassy to the Emperor Rudolph II. A violent opponent of the Roman church, he became one of the most vigorous of the Anglican controversialists against the Catholics, and he also shared his episcopal patron's hatred of nonconformists. His advocacy of Virginia colonization occurred in an important pulpit oration delivered on March 24, 1609, at Paul's Cross, in celebration of the anniversary of King James's coronation.[12] Printed a few weeks later as *A Sermon At The Solemnizing Of The Happie Inauguration of our most gracious and Religious Soueraigne King Iames. Wherein is manifestly proued, that the Soueraignty of Kings is immediately from God, and second to no authority on Earth whatsoeuer,* it is a piece of unadulterated flattery of the King, who is identified with Solomon. In proof of the sovereign's vast wisdom, Crakanthorpe pointed to the royal interest in the Virginia project, especially the "honourable expedition now happily intended"—an allusion to the fleet then being assembled under Sir Thomas Gates.[18] Although the tremendous theme of the King's wisdom left scant space for individual illustrations, the preacher inserted some eloquent passages on Virginia. "I may not stay in this straightnes of time," he declares, "to mention, much lesse set

96

forth vnto you, the great and manifold benefits which may redound to this our so populous a Nation, by planting an English Colony in a Territory as large and spacious almost as is England, and in a soyle so rich, fertill, and fruitefull, as that besides the sufficiencyes it naturally yealds for it selfe, may with best conuenience, supply some of the greatest wantes and necessities of these Kingdomes." Swept away by the contemplation of the benefits of westward expansion, Crakanthorpe almost forgets the heathen but remembers them in time to mention the benefits of salvation and to assure his audience of the profits to all "who shall be the meanes or furtherers of so happy a worke, not only to see a new Britaine in another world, but to heare also those, as yet Heathen, Barbarous, and Brutish people, together with our English, to learne the speech and language of Canaan." [14]

Not long after Crakanthorpe's enthusiastic encomium, listeners at Paul's Cross heard another commendation of Virginia, by George Benson, sometime fellow of Queen's College, Oxford. His deliverance, given at the command of the Bishop of London, was published as *A Sermon Preached At Paules Cross The Seaventh Of May, M.DC.IX* (1609). Less impressed than Crakanthorpe with the material benefits to be obtained, Benson nevertheless foresees the spread of the gospel westward, making of Virginia "a well watered garden." Reminding his congregation of the cruelties of the Spaniards, as related by Las Casas, he hopes that Englishmen will be more humane. [15]

Another preacher who espoused the cause of Virginia in the spring of 1609 was Robert Tynley, like Symonds a

fellow of Magdalen College, Oxford. Although his commendation was spontaneous and apparently not a part of
the official propaganda, Tynley makes his motive clear. He
was moved by intense hatred of the Roman church. His
praise of Virginia was uttered from the pulpit in the
churchyard of St. Mary's Spittle on April 17 and was published shortly thereafter in *Two Learned Sermons. The
one, of the mischievous subtiltie, and barbarous crueltie,
the other of the false Doctrines, and refined Haeresies of
the Romish Synagogue* (1609). In his Spittle sermon,
Tynley demonstrates the value of reducing the American
Indians to civil society and the Protestant faith. If that is
done, he asserts, "wee may with Gods blessing assuredly
expect the fruits which vsually accompany such godly enterprises; as are the honour of his Maiestie, whose name
shall by this meanes be glorious vnto the ends of the world,
the enlarging and further strengthening of his Realmes
and Dominions, the easing of this Land, which euen groan-
eth vnder the burden and numbers of her inhabitants, the
plentifull enriching of our selues and our Country with
such commodities as she now laboureth with the penury of
them." [16]

Tynley was known in his day as a learned divine and a
bitter enemy of papists. His observations on Virginia, im-
bedded in a diatribe against Rome, are further evidence of
the concerted effort of a group of Protestant pulpit orators
to arouse England to the danger of allowing Spain to
monopolize America. An immediate cause for much of the
discussion of colonization during the spring of 1609 may
be found in the widespread interest in Gates's expedition—

which finally sailed, with nine vessels, from Falmouth on June 8 [17]—but the zeal of ministers like Tynley, and, indeed, the purpose behind the official propaganda, went beyond the success or failure of a single expedition.

The campaign waged by the clergy in 1609 came to a climax in the following year with the publication of a famous sermon by William Crashaw, then preacher at the Inner Temple. The long title explains its subject matter: *A Sermon Preached In London before the right honorable the Lord LaWarre, Lord Gouernour and Captaine Generall of Virginea, and others of his Maiesties Counsell for that Kingdome, and the rest of the Aduenturers in that Plantation. At The Said Lord Generall His leaue taking of England his Natiue Countrey, and departure for Virginea, Febr. 21, 1609 [1610]. . . . Wherein both the lawfulnesse of that Action is maintained, and the necessity thereof is also demonstrated, not so much out of the grounds of Policie, as of Humanity, Equity, and Christianity. Taken from his mouth, and published by direction.* The work was edited by one L. D., who dedicated it to Parliament out of consideration for their zealous care to propagate the gospel. Although Crashaw insists that the conversion of the Indians is a "necessarie dutie," he is careful to emphasize the economic and political implications of colonization.

Hints of collaboration with other preachers and publicists appear in Crashaw's work. He repeats arguments in earlier pamphlets on Virginia and refers directly to Symonds' "learned and godly sermon" and to another "iudicious and sincere declaration, well pend, both set out

99

by authoritie," [18] which prove the lawfulness of England's efforts to establish plantations in America. The latter pamphlet was *A True And Sincere declaration of the purpose and ends of the Plantation begun in Virginia . . . Set forth by the authority of the Gouernors and Councellors established for that Plantation* (1610), which was hot from the press when Crashaw sat down to pen his own apologia.[19] Later in the year another *True Declaration* defending the colony against libelers was published by the Virginia Company. The pious Sir Edwin Sandys is supposed to have been mainly responsible for the preparation of these declarations, but they are so religious in tone that it is hard to believe that even he did not have the collaboration of Crashaw or some other preacher. At any rate, shortly afterward Crashaw was serving as a sort of director of publicity for the company.[20] He was not altogether disinterested, for he was listed among those who received the charter of 1609.

From the point of view of the Protestant expansionists, Crashaw was eminently fitted for his task. Best remembered now as the father of Richard Crashaw, the Catholic poet, in his time he was one of the most active opponents of Rome. At St. John's, Cambridge, he acquired a reputation for learning and, in many controversial works, demonstrated a profound knowledge of the church fathers. Two years before his espousal of Virginia he had printed *The Sermon Preached At the Crosse, Feb. xiiij. 1607 . . . Iustified by the Authour, both against Papist, and Brownist, to be the truth* (1608), a philippic of 173 pages condemning Catholics and noncomformists with equal severity.

Here, indeed, was a man whose conservative and godly views could be expected to inspire the confidence of Virginia Company officials and shareholders.

Crashaw's sermon on Virginia repeats the familiar arguments for colonization and adds a few new ideas. Virginia is another Land of Canaan, flowing with milk and honey, but in this era God does not want the Canaanites killed as of old. Instead, the Indians are to be converted, to become a benefit and a blessing to the English. Profits, Crashaw maintains, are not the principal end of the enterprise, but, if Englishmen carry out Jehovah's plans, He will be their principal ally and friend, and profits will follow as a natural consequence. Speaking directly to Lord Delaware, the preacher urges him to remember that he is "a Generall of Englishmen, nay a Generall of Christian men," who is destined to win a new realm for England and the God of Protestants.[21] To keep serpents of discord from the Eden on the James River, Crashaw would exclude all papists, stage players, and dissenters—a medley of folk whom he hated most heartily. "Suffer no Brownists, nor factious Separatists," he warns; "let them keepe their conuenticles elsewhere: let them goe and conuert some other Heathen."[22] The principal enemies of plantations, he insists, are "the Diuell, Papists, and Players," all of whom mock at religion and abuse the holy Scriptures.[23] Stage players, treated with particular venom, are accused of ridiculing the colony, spreading lies, and meddling with affairs of state. Crashaw may be referring to *Eastward Hoe*, by Chapman, Jonson, and Marston, acted and printed in 1605, for it has a scene satirizing Virginia.[24] References to Virginia, both favorable and unfavorable, occur frequently in the later drama. Some of the masques give a romantic portrayal of the Indians and of the riches of the country, which could not have been displeasing. In August, 1623, however, the Master of the Revels licensed to the company at the Curtain Theatre "A Tragedy of the Plantation of Virginia; the profaneness to be left out, otherwise not tolerated." [25] This play evidently described the massacre of 1622 and gave the colony precisely the sort of publicity least likely to attract investors or settlers. But whether the players had committed some overt act against Virginia at the time of Crashaw's outburst is not clear from surviving evidence; perhaps he is merely venting his ministerial spleen against the idlers of the theater, whom he hoped to see barred irrevocably from the promised land across the sea.

Crashaw was the first to perceive the influence that frontier life would exert on Englishmen. He foresees a moral and spiritual regeneration brought about by the rugged existence in the wilderness. Englishmen have grown soft in these latter days, he complains, and what their ancestors won with labor they "with idlenes haue lost." The frontier will not be hospitable to sloth, daintiness, and effeminacy, he declares, but rather it will bring out the strength in men and purge away the corruptions that ease has induced.[26] In short, Crashaw extols the colonial venture as "a most lawfull, an honorable, and a holy action." [27] And, like the other preachers, he shows the need for a Protestant bulwark in North America against the threat of Catholic domination of Spain from the south.

Crashaw had insisted, as one might expect a preacher to

do, that the principal aim of colonization in Virginia was the conversion of the heathen and the creation of a Protestant realm in opposition to the papists. But more significant is the same assertion, with even greater emphasis, in the two official *Declarations* published by the company in 1610. Whatever the private motives of these businessmen, and however greedy they may have been for profits, it is worthy of note that they placed pious arguments first in the propaganda with which they sought to influence public opinion. In *A True And Sincere declaration* they were careful to emphasize that the "Principall and Maine Ends . . . weare first to preach, & baptize into Christian Religion, and by propagation of the Gospell, to recouer out of the armes of the Diuell, a number of poore and miserable soules. . . . Secondly, to prouide and build vp for the publike Honour and safety of our gratious King and his Estates . . . some small Rampier of our owne, in this opportune and generall Summer of peace [by transplanting part of the surplus population to Virginia, and] . . . by this prouision they may bee seated as a Bulwarke of defence, in a place of aduantage, against a stranger enemy . . . which cannot choose but threaten vs, if wee consider, and compare the ends, ambitions, and practises, of our neighbour Countries, with our owne." [28] Last to be considered are the immediate profits from the commodities of the region. The asserted goal of the Virginia Company was "the foundation of a Common-wealth" [29] in the New World—a Protestant nation which would serve as a vent for the excess population at home and become a rampart against the common enemy, Spain.

The same arguments are repeated in *A True Declaration Of The estate of the Colonie in Virginia* (1610), published a few months after the first *Declaration*. The authority of Origen, Tertullian, Tacitus, and other worthies from the Christian and classical worlds is invoked in defense of colonies. Through other documents sponsored by the Virginia Company in the same period,[30] whether written by clergy or laymen, runs the identical theme of the Christian and patriotic purpose in the settlements overseas.

The disasters which overtook the Gates expedition and the subsequent starving time in the colony made necessary some justification of colonization beyond the appeal of immediate profits. The sermons delivered in 1609–10 and printed by order of the company must have helped to restore confidence in the scheme and allay unrest among the shareholders, for investors continued to pour money into the venture, and grumbling about the lack of profits diminished. Although investors may not have relished the notion of waiting for their reward in heaven, they at least became less vocal, or their complaints were smothered by pious logic.

Although the pace of ministerial propaganda slackened after the crisis of 1609–10, the loyalty of the clergy did not diminish and they remained useful advocates of the Virginia Company's projects.

A personal narrative of one of the first missionaries to Virginia was published by the company in 1613 as an antidote to slanders being "blowen abroad by Papists, Players, and such like."[31] The author was Alexander Whitaker and the document bore the cheering title of *Good Newes From*

Virginia. Sent To The Counsell and Company of Virginia, resident in England. . . . Perused and published by direction from that Counsell. The official who had read the manuscript and prepared it for printing was William Crashaw; he improved the opportunity by equipping it with a dedication almost as long as Whitaker's essay.

Misfortunes had beset the colony, Crashaw admits, but the failure of the devil, with all his machinations, to destroy the undertaking is a clear indication "that assuredly God himselfe is the founder, and fauorer of this Plantation." [32] In proof he offers four evidences of divine intercession: the miraculous deliverance of Sir Thomas Gates and Sir George Somers after their shipwreck in the Bermudas; the discovery through their shipwreck that the Bermudas were a fair garden spot set aside for the English; the providential arrival of Gates and Somers at Jamestown in time to rescue the starving settlers; and the eagerness of English investors to subscribe large sums "without any certaine or apparant hope of speedie profit." Thus Crashaw turns disasters into a demonstration of Providence working "to some higher end then ordinary." [33] To a question on everyone's lips at the moment as to why Lord Delaware did not return to Virginia, the apologist replies that the explanation is the present failure of fainthearted folk to assist in "so holy and honorable a worke." [34]

By way of introducing the author, Master Whitaker, Crashaw takes occasion to point out that the preachers selected to go to Virginia have been substantial men of learning, not bankrupts. Whitaker, a master of arts of Cambridge, was possessed of a competence, and had been moved to cast his lot with the colonists by a desire to share in a great Christian enterprise. These Virginia preachers are apostles carrying the gospel into Macedonia.[35]

When Crashaw finally allows the reader to come to Whitaker's part of the book, we once more discover familiar proofs from Scripture of the advantages of colonizing. Though profits have not yet been realized, the preacher assures his audience that they are inevitable. To doubt the ultimate outcome is to doubt the promises of God. He begins with a text from Ecclesiastes 11:1, "Cast thy bread vpon the waters: for after many daies thou shalt finde it," and delivers a homily on liberality. Money subscribed to the Virginia Company will become treasure stored in heaven, with the further advantage of profits usable in this world. Whitaker gives a luscious picture of the fruitfulness of Virginia and appeals to English sportsmen by describing the rare sport to be had from fishing with an angle. Indeed, fishermen will find there a paradise: "The Riuers abound with Fish both small and great: . . . Shads of a great bignesse, and Rock-fish follow them. Trouts, Base [bass], Flounders, and other daintie fish come in before the other bee gone: then come multitudes of great Sturgeons. . . . I cannot reckon nor giue proper names to the diuers kinds of fresh fish in our riuers; I haue caught with mine angle, Pike, Carpe, Eele, Perches of six seuerall kinds, Crea-fish [crayfish] and the Torope or little Turtle, besides many smaller kinds."[36] The land wants nothing, Whitaker proves, to make it another England, pleasant and bountiful beyond the imaginations of men.

The change in the management of the Virginia Company

in 1619, when Sir Edwin Sandys succeeded Sir Thomas Smythe as treasurer, did not alter the official emphasis on religion. Both factions, as we have seen, shared similar religious beliefs and hated and opposed Spain.[37] Although ministerial propaganda was somewhat less blatant during Sandys' administration, it was by no means neglected, and the air of piety at the meetings of the company court was probably accentuated.

Sandys was little short of a preacher himself. The son of the Archbishop of York, he had taken orders at Oxford and had advised Richard Hooker concerning *Of the Laws of Ecclesiastical Polity*. He himself had written *A Relation Of The State Of Religion* (1605), which described, with a detachment unusual in that age, the sects of western Europe. The manuscript of this book was prepared for a private audience, and when it was published without his knowledge Sandys requested the Court of High Commission to call it in and order it burned. He was also the author of a paraphrase of the Psalms, set to music by Robert Tailor and published as *Sacred Hymns. Consisting Of Fifti Select Psalms Of David and others* (1615). His powers of religious persuasion were such that he is said to have converted the Earl of Southampton from popery.

Associated with Sandys were two brothers, John and Nicholas Ferrar, whose reputation for piety exceeded even his.[38] These three earnest Anglicans were the dominating influences in the Virginia Company from 1619 until the dissolution in 1624. Not only their personal faith, but also a belief that Catholic Spain was actively hostile to Virginia, profoundly affected their policies. Like many others in

England, they were convinced that colonization in Virginia would be one safeguard against the ambition of Spain for world domination. Their belief that a strong colony must be established as quickly as possible accounts for an almost frantic campaign to enlist emigrants, even the Puritan separatists of Leyden, who dickered with Sandys concerning land in Virginia.

One of the first actions of Sandys after becoming treasurer was to propose the allocation of land at Henrico for the use of a college "for the trayning and bringing vp of Infidells children to the true knowledge of God & vnderstanding of righteousnes." [39] King James had already authorized the bishops to collect money throughout England for this purpose. Sandys also proposed to send over fifty emigrants to work the land. A few months later, the treasurer expressed grave concern over the scarcity of ministers in Virginia and suggested a plan to send "one sufficient Deuine to each of those Burroughs, for the Comfort of the soules of the inhabitants, by preachinge and expoundinge the word of God vnto them." [40] Although Sandys, like other officers of the Virginia Company, was desirous of dividends for the shareholders, he regarded the firm establishment of a Christian commonwealth as the first essential, even of material success.

Plans to supply the colony with schools and preachers continued to occupy the minds of Sandys and his colleagues. [41] In 1621 they received the aid of Patrick Copland a zealous preacher of the East India Company, who took up a collection of more than £70 on board the ship "Royal James" as a contribution toward the foundation of

a free school in Virginia. Copland henceforth became an
enthusiastic advocate of the American colony, and for his
pains received three shares of stock in the company.

Invited to preach in Bow Church before the company on
April 18, 1622, Copland delivered such an optimistic and
colorful discourse that a month later it was sent to the
printers and appeared as *Virginia's God be Thanked, Or
A Sermon Of Thanksgiving For The Happie successe of
the affayres in Virginia this last yeare. . . . And now published by the Commandement of the said honorable Company*. The author was already experienced in the ways of
the East India Company and knew the kind of thing that
would please the Virginia officials. It is not surprising,
therefore, that his account is rosy to the point of hyperbole
when he describes the richness of the new country, a vast
Eden, empty save for a few heathen—a realm waiting to
be settled. "Our Countrey aboundeth with people," he
points out; "your Colony wanteth them. You all know
that there is nothing more dangerous for the estate of Com-
monwealths then when the people doe increase to a greater
number and multitude then may iustly parallel with the
largenesse of the place and country in which they liue." [42]
To save England from the calamity of overpopulation,
God had reserved this great country vacant until now. The
author contrasts the opportunities abroad with the poverty
and distress at home. Such misfortunes as had previously
befallen the colony were merely evidence of God's judg-
ments upon the idle sinners who made up the first supply
of settlers, but these have already been punished and Providence will henceforth bless the enterprise. No longer need

emigrants be troubled by hunger, pestilence, and inconveniences in their dwelling places. Moreover, there is such "a happie league of Peace and Amitie soundly concluded and faithfully kept, betweene the English and the Natiues, that the feare of killing each other is now vanished away." [43] Ironically, when Copland was uttering these words, news of the disastrous massacre of March 22, 1622, was already on its way to England.

Bad news travels fast, and the Stationers' Company on July 10 registered for printing a pamphlet entitled *Mourninge Virginia*, and on September 11 a poem on *The Late massacre in Virginia*.[44] Sir Edwin Sandys felt that conditions demanded a sermon by one of the most famous preachers of England to counteract such unfavorable publicity, and he invited Dr. John Donne, dean of St. Paul's, to address the Virginia Company on November 13. Within a few weeks Donne's contribution was in print as *A Sermon Vpon The VIII. Verse Of The I. Chapter Of The Acts Of The Apostles* (1622). In his dedication to members of the company, Donne confesses that he has been commanded to publish the work. "By your fauours," he says, "I had some place amongst you before: but now I am an Aduenturer; if not to Virginia, yet for Virginia; for euery man that Prints, Aduentures. For the Preaching of this Sermon, I was but vnder your Inuitation. . . . But for the Printing of this Sermon, I am not onely vnder your Inuitation, but vnder your Commandement. . . . The first was an act of Loue, this, of Iustice." Verily Donne was an adventurer, for he had been made free of the company and of the council on July 3, 1622, and now had a stake in the success of the plantation.[45]

The sermon is not one of Dr. Donne's happiest examples of prose, but one striking paragraph was prophetic: "You shall haue made this Iland, which is but as the Suburbs of the old world, a Bridge, a Gallery to the new; to ioyne all to that world that shall neuer grow old, the Kingdome of heauen. You shall add persons to this Kingdome, and to the Kingdome of heauen, and adde names to the Bookes of our Chronicles, and to the Booke of Life." After extolling the efforts to establish a colony in the New World, Donne points out that the papists are bitterly hostile to Protestant expansion in America. In a letter to Sir Thomas Roe on December 1, 1622, he reports details of the sermon and expresses his dislike of the proposed marriage of Prince Charles to the Infanta of Spain.[46] The threatened union of a Catholic princess with the heir to the English throne gave further impetus to the clergy's desire for a curtailment of Spanish power overseas. Donne's sermon illustrates the confusion of religious, economic, and political motives of the time. If it proved too metaphysical for the comprehension of some of his readers, the dean's prestige was so great that his endorsement was worth all it cost the company.[47] Further evidence of Donne's zeal for Virginia appears in a poem written in commendation of Captain John Smith's *The Generall Historie Of Virginia* (1624) and prefixed to that work. According to the gossip of the day, Donne had long hoped to become secretary of the Virginia Company.[48]

Concerning the effect on public opinion of the sponsorship of Virginia by the clergy, we can only guess. Obviously, piety alone did not persuade Sir Thomas Smythe and Sir Edwin Sandys to draw the preachers into the service of the company. Evidently the men of commerce were convinced of the preachers' practical utility as well as of their influence with the Almighty. Of one thing we can be certain: when King James took over the affairs of the Virginia Company in 1624, the public had already become so convinced of the value of the colony that not even such dramatic disasters as the massacre of 1622 could prevent their continued support. And presently Englishmen learned that the promises of the men of God were true. Thanks to the craving for tobacco and the productivity of the soil on the banks of the James, investors began to make money, and Virginia became an established commonwealth of English Protestants. The preachers had an important influence in maintaining morale until this development took place.

The notion that God had especially reserved certain areas for English settlement, repeated so often in connection with Virginia, was advanced by both laymen and clergymen in recommendation of other regions. A little later, of course, it became a cardinal belief of the Puritans of New England. But, in the period we are considering, advocates of Guiana and Bermuda maintained the theory of providential care for English settlements.

The promoter Robert Harcourt, for example, asserted in 1613 that the "rich & mighty Empire of Guiana" had remained unconquered by the Spaniards because "the powerfull hand of God doth worke for vs in this behalfe, and hath reserued the execution of this action for the honour of our Nation." [49] The welfare of the nation and the glory of God dictate that Englishmen establish a nation there in opposition to Spain, Harcourt adds.[50]

Another emphatic assertion of divine intercession to preserve land in the Western Hemisphere for the English came from the Reverend Lewis Hughes, one of the first two ministers sent to the Bermudas, or the Somers Islands, when the colony was still under the control of Sir Thomas Smythe and the Virginia Company. Hughes evidently had instructions to write about the excellent qualities of that tropical paradise, and in 1615 appeared *A Letter, Sent into England from the Summer Ilands. Written by Mr. Lewes Hughes, Preacher of Gods Word.* The author, who had attained some notoriety in 1602 for exorcising witches,[51] was careful to point out that the previous bad reputation of these islands for enchantment and devils was merely part of the divine plan. As cherubim had been placed to watch the Garden of Eden, so "God hath terrified and kept all people of the world from comming into these Ilands to inhabit them." In gratitude for "the goodnes of Almighty God, in keeping these Ilands secret, . . . till now that it hath pleased his holy Maiesty to discouer and bestow them vpon his people of England," Hughes thinks only pious settlers should come to the new Eden.[52] As another proof of God's care for the safety of the English colonists, Hughes describes the natural fortifications and the excellent harbors which could be easily defended.[53] In a second pamphlet, *A Plaine And True Relation Of The Goodnes Of God towards the Sommer Ilands* (1621), the preacher further emphasized "the goodnes of God, in reseruing and keeping these Ilands, euer since the beginning of the world, for the English Nation, and in not discouering them to any, to inhabit but to the English." [54] Providential also was the creation of two fine harbors "with such curious & narrow comming in, as [a] few men in the Plat-formes and Forts on both sides the Channels are able (by the helpe of God) to sinke all Ships of Enemies that shall offer to come in." The fearful rocks and shoals which environ the islands make them "as safe from forraine inuasion," Hughes declares, "as any people in the world, which is a great comfort." [55] These are the harbors and bases in which English-speaking peoples even yet hope to find great comfort.

Throughout the reign of James the clergy with scarcely a dissenting voice furthered the propaganda for expansion into the New World. Upon that topic Protestants of whatever sect could agree. The unanimous hatred of Catholic Spain, which came to a climax in 1623 with an outburst from the clergy over the marriage alliance planned for Prince Charles, gave particular point to their consistent arguments for Protestant colonies overseas. Virginia was the first answer to their prayers. The clergy, with the horror of domination by the Spanish Catholic empire ever present in their minds, perceived more clearly than others the significance of that beginning of a counter-empire. Englishmen would occupy the new Canaan and would presently wax strong and smite the hosts of popery entrenched to the south. With such conviction did they preach this doctrine that Englishmen at length accepted it as their imperial destiny.

CHAPTER FIVE

Samuel Purchas
and the Heathen

ON A SUMMER'S day in 1797, the Reverend Samuel Taylor Coleridge sought relief from the toothache by taking a dose of opium and reading the works of his brother cleric, the Reverend Samuel Purchas. From the modern point of view, one could hardly find a book better calculated to put one to sleep than *Purchas his Pilgrimage* (1613), the volume which Coleridge selected. But, before the poet fell asleep, he discovered in his reading enough wonders to inspire a poetical vision which took the form of a marvelous piece of imagery known to us as "Kubla Khan." Long before Coleridge's time, Purchas' work had stirred the imaginations of Englishmen and kindled in them an interest in the expanding world and the customs and beliefs of heathen peoples in lands till then unknown. King James I made the book "Ordinarie of his Bed chamber," the author boasted, and read it through seven times [1]—no mean task, even for the English Solomon, because the first edition ran to 752 folio pages. Subsequent editions were expanded, and the fourth, published in 1626, was swelled to 967 pages, plus three additional treatises by way of appendix.

The *Pilgrimage,* which aroused the enthusiasm of King James and his contemporaries and furnished Coleridge with a theme for poetry, is scarcely known today. Purchas is remembered better for his vast compilation of travels entitled *Hakluytus Posthumus or Purchas His Pilgrimes* (1625), a work so similar in title to his earlier book that the *Pilgrimage* and the *Pilgrimes* are frequently confused. Both influenced their age, and, though we may have forgotten their prolix author and undiscriminating editor, his contemporaries valued him, and the East India Company and the Virginia Company rewarded him tangibly for his services to English expansion.

Samuel Purchas was first and last a preacher. His curiosity about the spiritual state of the heathen led him to explore history, to examine the narratives of travelers, and to write the *Pilgrimage,* which dwelt morbidly on the abominations and iniquities of unchristian folk. The subtitle of the work promised a relation "Of The World And The Religions Observed In All Ages And places discouered, from the Creation vnto this Present. . . . With briefe Descriptions of the Countries, Nations, States, Discoueries, Priuate and Publike Customes, and the most Remarkable Rarities of Nature, or Humane Industrie, in the same." Among other purposes professed by the author, in his dedication to George Abbot, Archbishop of Canterbury, was the intention of displaying "the Paganisme of Antichristian Poperie, and other Pseudo-Christian heresies, and

116

the Truth of Christianitie as it is now professed and established in our Church." The resultant mixture of geography, religion, and refutation of popery was pleasing to the
archbishop, who had written somewhat in that kind himself.
Accordingly, Purchas, who until then had held a living in
the unwholesome air of Essex, received a post as Abbot's
chaplain and immediately thereafter became rector of St.
Martin's, Ludgate. More than that, the book established
Purchas' reputation for learning and brought him to the
notice of Richard Hakluyt,[2] whose literary heir he became.
The *Pilgrimage* was probably the means by which Purchas
also attracted the attention of Sir Edwin Sandys, for
Sandys' own religious geography of Europe gave the two
men a common interest. At any rate, in 1622 Sandys had
Purchas admitted to the Virginia Company, where he
served in some sort of advisory capacity.[3]

In the preparation of the *Pilgrimage*, Purchas combed
histories, ancient and modern, and read voraciously in the
literature of travel, including Hakluyt's great compilation.
More of a journalist than a scholar, he knew the sort of
thing that would titillate the interest of his day. Indeed,
the *Pilgrimage* is a remarkable reflection of the popular
taste of Jacobean England for encyclopedic knowledge derived from history, religion, and travel. Here in a single
book was a medley of fascinating details about the history,
habitats, and beliefs of strange peoples. For instance, the
section on America begins with a running account of the
discovery and explorations of the New World, and, after
a description of "the rare Creatures therein found," proceeds to a more detailed exposition of the geography, his-

tory, and religion of particular regions. Such a work could not fail to please readers who were equally avid for information about the wonders of the New World and the way to the New Jerusalem. Furthermore, to an age that loved the signs and symbols of erudition, the copious notes with which Purchas filled the margins proved reassuring. The publication of four editions of so large and expensive a book between 1613 and 1626 is proof of its popularity.

In the description of Virginia, Purchas took occasion to insert a defense of the colony against its libelers. "Thus haue I beene bold somewhat largely to relate the proceedings of this Plantation," he remarks, "to supplant such slanders and imputations as some haue conceiued or receiued against it, and to excite the diligence and industrie of all men of abilitie, to put to their helping hand in this action, so honourable in it selfe, glorious to God in the furtherance of his truth, and beneficiall to the common-wealth, and to the priuate purses of the Aduenturers, if the blooming of our hopes bee not blasted with our negligence." [4]

In concluding a general chapter on the north parts of the New World, Purchas appends a prayer to Almighty God that the Virginia plantation "may triumph in her conquests of Indian Infidels, maugre the bragges of that Adulteresse [Spain] that vaunteth her selfe to be the only Darling of God and Nature." [5] Although Purchas is cautious about meddling in dangerous matters of state, he does not hesitate to suggest that Englishmen must circumvent the encroachment of Spanish Catholics in distant regions. He gives emphasis to that thesis by concluding the whole work with a bitter indictment of Spanish Catholics for their cruelties to the Indians. The *Pilgrimage* thus echoes the unanimous voice of the Protestant clergy in warning against the colonial monopoly of Spain.

The *Pilgrimage* was an important piece of oblique propaganda for colonial expansion. If Purchas had a consuming zeal to preach this gospel in the *Pilgrimage*—as Hakluyt had been motivated in his labors—he did not reveal it, but nevertheless he included many incidental observations on the need for Englishmen to occupy a portion of heathendom. And, what was more important, his descriptions of foreign lands and peoples stirred his readers to further interest in the world outside of England.

When Hakluyt died in 1616, his mantle fell on the shoulders of Samuel Purchas, who wore the habiliments with more delight than grace. Hakluyt was a scholar of genuine scientific interest, a thinker with a clear perception of his duty in helping to formulate a national policy that had in it the seeds of imperial development. Purchas was a country parson more interested, as he himself said, "in by-wayes then high-wayes." [6] But, though he had neither the intellect nor the editorial discrimination of Hakluyt, he continued Hakluyt's great task of compiling voyage literature, and published in 1625 *Hakluytus Posthumus or Purchas His Pilgrimes,* a work whose title suggested the editor's debt to his predecessor.

The *Pilgrimes* was an imposing compilation of four vast folio volumes bearing dedications to Prince Charles, the Duke of Buckingham, the Bishop of Lincoln, and the Archbishop of Canterbury. In the course of his labors, the editor's notions of expansion underwent a marked development. Whereas in the *Pilgrimage* his comments on colonial activities had been more or less incidental, in the *Pilgrimes* he shows a definite purpose to promote ideas of colonization and overseas trade. In his dedication to Prince Charles, he waves the flag with the fervor of an ardent imperialist and delights to use the new word "Great Britain" to describe the realm at home. In the twenty books of the *Pilgrimes*, Purchas assures the Prince, are the records of "the English Martialist everywhere following armes, whiles his Countrey is blessed at home with Beati Pacifici; the Merchant coasting more Shoares and Ilands for commerce, then his Progenitors have heard off, or himselfe can number; the Mariner making other seas a Ferry, and the widest Ocean a Strait, to his discovering attempts; wherein wee joy to see Your Highnesse to succeed Your Heroike Brother, in making the furthest Indies by a New Passage neerer to Great Britaine. Englands out of England are here presented, yea Royal Scotland, Ireland, and Princely Wales, multiplying new Scepters to His Majestie and His Heires in a New World."

The notion of imperial grandeur implied in these words was pleasing to the royal house and to thousands of Englishmen who had been gradually losing their insularity as they learned more of the wonders of the great world. The *Pilgrimes* appeared before King James's death, and Purchas presented the volumes in person to the monarch, who expressed great interest in the work, "which," says Purchas, "he made his Nightly taske, till God called him by fatall sicknesse to a better Pilgrimage." On the very day of his death, the King sent Purchas "a fauorable message of his gentle approbation and incouragement." [7] Readers less highly placed also approved the sentiments and the matter of the *Pilgrimes*. The East India Company, for example, expressed their satisfaction by a gift of £100 and took three sets of books, as the court minutes explain: "Mr. Purchas, a preacher and Bachelor of Divinity, presented the Court with four volumes containing many several treatises of the Indies and other remote parts of the world, having formerly presented the same unto his Majesty and the Prince, wherein is recorded particularly the many discoveries made by this Company, together with the great benefit which this kingdom reapeth thereby. Also he presented an epistle to the Company, which he read to them and demanded whether they were willing it should be inserted in some convenient place of this history. The Court took in very thankful part his labours, and in token of their good acceptance thereof gratified him with 100 l., and the Company to have three sets of his books." [8]

Purchas' relations with the East India Company indicate his increased enthusiasm for the doctrine of expansion. In another appearance before the company court, he declared his purpose in compiling the *Pilgrimes* to have been "the glory of God and honour of this nation," and he added significantly that, if he could be of further service, he hoped "they would make use of him as of a man obliged to the Company." [9] The epistle that he had previously expressed a desire to print was an indictment of the Dutch for their treatment of the English in the East Indies, particularly for the massacre at Amboina in 1623, and was intended to arouse the English nation to take a firm stand against hostile Dutch commanders in the Orient. The East India Company was anxious to publish this piece of propaganda in the *Pilgrimes*, but both the printer and the bookbinder demurred. Finally, on January 26, 1625, "the Court resolved to let it rest for awhile, and if they cannot procure it to be bound with the book, they will print it upon some other occasions." [10] No record exists of the printing of the controversial epistle. Extant copies of the *Pilgrimes* contain "A Note touching the Dutch" (immediately following the preface to the first volume), in which Purchas mentions the massacre at Amboina and other iniquities of the Dutch. However, descriptions, in the text, of the hostility of the Dutch to the East India Company are not meant, he explains, as a condemnation of the whole Dutch nation—who, after all, are fellow Protestants—but as an exposure of certain wicked commanders.

The influence of the *Pilgrimes*, coupled with that of the *Pilgrimage*, was enormous. As in his earlier work, Purchas combined the qualities of journalist, preacher, geographer, and propagandist, and reached a wider public than Hakluyt had known. Modern scholars have berated the parson of St. Martin's for his failure to preserve scientific details, for throwing away data in ships' logs, for abbreviating narratives, and for other editorial practices contrasting unfavorably with Hakluyt's, but they forget that Purchas feared tediousness as the devil and sought to reduce the vast body of travel literature to a compass acceptable to the general reader. He was a popularizer with a purpose. Like Hakluyt before him, he sought to arouse the English public to a sense of their obligation to go forth and seize a portion of the fallow world beyond the seas. If he showed a greater preoccupation with the foibles of the heathen and the need to evangelize them after the use of St. Martin's, Ludgate, it simply proves that Purchas was a typical Jacobean, reflecting the ideas and the tastes of his own day.

Scattered through the *Pilgrimes* are many editorial observations emphasizing the need for expansion overseas, but the climax of Purchas' propaganda comes in an original essay concluding the Tenth Book. It bears the descriptive title of "Virginias Verger: Or a Discourse shewing the benefits which may grow to this Kingdome from American English Plantations, and specially those of Virginia and Summer Ilands." Probably because the essay is buried among an infinite number of travel narratives, its importance has been entirely overlooked. Yet Purchas reveals himself here as something more than a parson with missionary instincts. His essay is a reasoned and persuasive argument for expansion, written with the fervor of religious conviction.

Being a preacher, Purchas could not forbear to cast his argument in the form of a sermon, beginning with the pious observation that "God is the beginning and end, the Alpha and Omega, that first and last, of whom and for whom are all things. The first and last thing therefore in this Virginian argument considerable is God; that is, whether we have Commission from him to plant, and whether the Plantation may bring glory to him." Filling his margins with a panoply of texts from the Scriptures, he demonstrates conclusively that the undertaking is particularly under the eye of God and that English Christians have an especial claim to tenure in the regions beyond the seas, "whereof Hypocrites [meaning Spanish Catholics] and Heathens are not capable." [11]

The question of the right of Englishmen to displace natives from their lands in the New World—even if they were heathen—troubled the consciences of strict moralists and constituted at least a theoretical stumbling block to colonization, which the expansionists believed should be removed. Other preachers before Purchas had discussed the matter, but he resolved this case of conscience with a greater array of biblical learning than any of his predecessors had produced. The bald theft of heathen lands would be wicked, Purchas admits. "The scope of the Virginian Plantation [is] not to make Savages and wild degenerate men of Christians," he emphasizes, "but Christians of those Savage, wild, degenerate men; to whom preaching must needs bee vaine, if it begins with publike Latrocinie." With the Anglo-Saxon genius for discovering high moral reasons to justify doubtful deeds, Purchas proves from the word of God and the law of nature that his countrymen have a perfect right to American soil, particularly Virginia and the Bermudas.

First, "as men we have a naturall right to replenish the whole earth." Since Virginia and the Bermudas are so barren of people that the sparse inhabitants cannot begin to make use of the land, settlers, "by Law of Nature and Humanitie, hath right of Plantation, and may not by other after-commers be dispossessed, without wrong to human nature." Civilized people are justified in occupying areas thinly populated by nomads, "where the people is wild, and holdeth no settled possession. Thus the holy Patriarks removed their habitations and pasturages, when those parts of the world were not yet replenished: and thus the whole world hath been planted and peopled with former and later Colonies: and thus Virginia hath roome enough for her own . . . and for others also which wanting at home, seeke habitations there in vacant places, with perhaps better right then the first, which (being like Cain, both Murtherers and Vagabonds in their whatsoever and howsoever owne) I can scarsly call Inhabitants." To question this right to settle savage countries would be not only to indict most nations, who have generally followed this practice, but "to disappoint also that Divine Ordinance of replenishing the Earth." [12]

A second powerful claim to portions of the New World is based on economic reasoning. Nations have a natural right of merchandise and trade. No single country has a right to everything, and God in his wisdom has diversified the commodities of the world so that trade between countries may flourish. "It is therefore ungodly, and inhumane also to deny the world to men, or like Manger-dogges . . . to prohibite that for others habitation, whereof themselves can make no use; or for merchandise, whereby much benefit accreweth to both parts." If savages, failing to observe these immutable laws of God and nature, prove "Outlawes of Humanity," then they expose themselves "to the chastisement of that common Law of mankind" as well as to "the Law of Nations," for they themselves are not "worthy of the name of a Nation." Thus civilized peoples may invade the lands of savages who retard human prog-

ress. Thus "David conquered all the Kingdome of the Am-
monites and left it to his successors in many generations." [18]
This ancient argument, derived from Hebrew and Roman
practice and theory, is the same that the German Reich in
a later day brought out and dusted off to justify aggression in Poland and other regions described as "backward."

Having laid a general foundation of law for the occupation of American soil, Purchas then proceeds to establish
English rights to Virginia and the Bermudas by virtue of
discoveries and settlement. He also sets forth seven honorable reasons why the colonization of Virginia commands
the support of all patriots. These seven reasons, as Purchas
describes them, are the glory of religion, the good of humanity, the honor of the English nation which "enjoyneth
us not basely to loose the glory of our forefathers acts,"
the honor of the King, the honor of the kingdom, the
profits to be obtained, and the necessity of finding an outlet for the surplus population of the homeland.

In describing the honor to the kingdom, Purchas indicates the imperial significance of overseas dominions: "As
Scotland and England seeme sisters, so Virginia, New England, New found Land in the Continent already planted
in part with English Colonies, together with Bermuda,
and other Ilands, may be the adopted and legall Daugh-
ters of England. An honorable designe, to which Honor
stretcheth her faire hand, the five fingers whereof are
adorned with such precious Rings, each enriched with in-
valuable Jewels of Religion, Humanity, Inheritance, the
King, the Kingdome." The models for this expansion are
found in antiquity and in contemporary history. The first

example was the Roman Empire, which "sowed Roman Colonies thorow the World, as the most naturall and artificiall way to win and hold the World Romaine." But nearer at hand and more obvious than the Roman dominion is the wide-reaching power of Spain, which grew into a rich empire after Columbus "stumbled upon a Westerne World whereof hee never dreamed." [14] If Rome and Spain could achieve imperial greatness, so can England. "And thus," he argues, "you have Virginias hopes in generall propounded by Spanish example, urged and enfourced by our necessity of seeking vent to such home-fulnesse." [15]

The natural situation of Virginia, its excellent climate, its magnificent rivers, its bays and harbors, its fisheries, its fertile soil, its great forests, its mines, and its abundance of all commodities required of man, make it a vast rich Eden waiting to supply the living space needed by the poor of England. If the nation would take advantage of these opportunities, the dreadful stagnation of trade at home could be alleviated, Purchas thinks. The scarcity of money, with ensuing evils, he maintains, "is in greatest part caused by the Merchandizes sought and bought in other Countries, whereby our Moneyes fall into forraine Whirle-pooles without hopes of recovery; whereas if our Trade lay (as we see the Spanish) with our owne Colonies and Plantations else-where, wee should hold them still current in our owne Nation, and draw others to bring to us both Wares and Moneyes from other Regions for the Commodities aforesaid." [16] In this sentence Purchas epitomizes the economic and political theories underlying the early development of the British Empire. Also worthy of note is the fact that the parson of St. Martin's was one of the first to hold up the examples of the Roman and Spanish empires for English imitation.

Not merely commercial prosperity but national defense required colonization overseas, Purchas is careful to point out. Indeed, he devotes some of his most earnest passages to the demonstration of that thesis. Virginia, particularly, is a valuable asset by reason of its naval stores and strategic position on the flank of the routes to the West Indies. "If an Iland needs woodden Wals to secure it from others, Virginia offers her service herein," he observes. "Yea, as England hath wooed and visited Virginia, so herein Virginia will be glad and rejoyce to visit England, in her there-built ships, and to dwell here with us in thence-brought Timbers." [17] A big navy is the source of world power, Purchas proves from history. "Yea, without a Navie, Salomon had not beene so meet a Type of Christ, so glorious in Domesticall, Politicall or Ecclesiasticall magnificence." Since the English Solomon now has Virginia to supply the materials for great ships, England can look forward to a new era of strength. "Haile then, al-haile Virginia," Purchas exclaims in pious ecstasy, "hope of our decayed Forrests, Nursery of our Timbers, second supply to our shipping." [18]

After further emphasis upon the value of Virginia as the arsenal of England, Purchas discusses the strategic reasons for developing strong bases in Virginia and the Bermudas. "I adde further," he says, "that the prosecution of the Virginian Plantation is both profitable and necessary for the strengthening of the Plantations already begun in Summer

Ilands, New England, and the New found Land, and that other expected in New Scotland." [19] Its central position on the lines of communication between the English colonies and its nearness to trade routes to the Spanish dominions, give it unusual importance. Moreover, if the long-hoped-for discovery of a new passage to the South Seas should be made, Virginia would be essential to the protection of English shipping in that trade. Since Spain and Portugal have attempted to monopolize trade with the Indies and treat all others as pirates, force is necessary to gain a rightful share in this commerce. "In the East, both English and Dutch have maintayned their just Trade by force, which by unjust force was denied, and have paid themselves largely for all losses sustayned by the Insultings or Assaultings of those Monopolians, with gaine with honour." [20] Purchas desires not to meddle too far in such matters, but King James, "he whose words and workes hath ever beene Beati pacifici, knowes best when and how to exact his and the Worlds right, in the World, of which God hath granted a Monopoly to no man." [21]

Shrewdly aware of King James's predilection for peace, Purchas skillfully shows that colonies in America may be necessary to the maintenance of peace in a world armed and ready to go to war. "The most certaine, honorable, and beauteous front of Peace, hath a backe part of Warre, and therefore in securest Peace, Prudence is not so secure, but she armeth herselfe against feares of War, forearming men by the Sword drawne to prevent the drawing of Swords, and eyther eschewes it, or reaps good out of it." [22] The security of England's trade, and England's independence of action in peace or war, require strong outposts for protection. "Once, in just and even peace, Virginia stands fit to become Englands Factor in America; if war should happen, both it and Bermuda are fit Sentinels and Scouts, yea fit Searchers and Customers, fit Watch-towers and Arsenals to maintaine right against all wrong-doers." [23] Here Purchas, almost in the words used by statesmen of our own day, warns England that she must be assured of the protection which Virginia and the Bermudas can give. In peace or war, he repeats, Virginia and Bermuda will be useful "to this Kingdome." Like Lewis Hughes, ten years before, he stresses the natural fortifications of the Bermudas, those rock-bound harbors able to "laugh at an Armada, at a World of Ships." [24] Virginia likewise is capable of defense against any hostile force, and "the worst of enemies to be feared is English backwardnesse or frowardnesse." [25]

To wake England from its complacent slumber and to counteract a stubborn refusal to discern the facts of geography—the "frowardnesse" complained of here—were Purchas' fixed purposes. He grows eloquent in his appeal: "If others impotence and importunities force a War, Virginia and Summer Ilands seeme to this English body as two American hands, eares, feete; two eyes for defence: two Keyes . . . for offence: two Armes to get, encompasse, embrace: two Fists to strike: the Sword and Dagger, Ship and Pinnace, Castle and Rampire, Canon & Musket, Arsenale and Peere, and whatsoever God shall please to give to humaine industry." These regions have been especially set aside for the English, who must not be asleep to their divinely appointed rights. "And although I am no Secretary of Gods Counsell for the Indies, yet event hath revealed thus much of his will, that no other Christian Nation hath yet gotten and maintained possession in those parts but the English: to whom therefore wee may gather their decreed serviceablenesse in Peace, advantagiousnesse in Warre, and opportunity for both, to be both Magazine and Bulwarke, and ready even by naturall scituation to sit on the skirts of whatsoever enemies, which passe from America to Europe." [26] In a peroration summarizing the infinite advantages of colonies overseas, Purchas addresses a prayer to "God the Father, Sonne and holy ghost" "that he may vouchsafe to goe with us, and we with him, and after him to Virginia." [27]

For its vision and wisdom, Purchas' essay is one of the best discussions, in this period, of the advantages of colonial expansion. It is a worthy successor to Hakluyt's *Discourse of Western Planting*. Although the author borrowed much from Master Hakluyt, his treatise shows that he too had done some original thinking, that he had pondered world maps with shrewd perception, and that he had become an intelligent apostle of geopolitics.

Originally written as a separate tractate, "at the request of some worthy friends," [28] the essay was probably prepared at the behest of the Virginia Company to counteract the bad news of the massacre of 1622. Purchas hints as much. Had it been published separately instead of being abridged and buried with countless other documents, it would have given Purchas a larger place among the advocates of empire.

When he finished his discourse on Virginia, the industrious parson had not yet said all that was on his mind concerning overseas expansion. The epilogue to the *Pilgrimes* once more returns to the argument. While flattering King James for his wisdom and magnificence, Purchas again waves the flag for national expansion. Under this mighty sovereign, the kingdom has grown great and prosperous, commerce has increased, and the superfluous population has been disposed, not by invasion of weaker neighbors, but by settlement in spacious America "to breed New Britaines in another World." In a fever of patriotic sentiment, Purchas is moved to boast that "at home doth Great Britain enjoy this Gem of Goodnes, the best part of the Ring of the worlds Greatnes." [29] After a final enumeration of the merits of Virginia, he concludes with a word of praise for both Virginia and New England; concerning the latter he rejoices "to heare (by one lately returned thence, Master Morell, a Minister and man of credit) that the affaires of New England are thriving and hopefull, which two Colonies of Virginia and New England (with all their Neighbours) God make as Rachel and Leah." [30] The final portions of the *Pilgrimes* were devoted to narratives of exploration in the northern parts of America. Had the indefatigable compiler been vouchsafed a few more years of industry, he undoubtedly would have composed a tractate on the virtues of New England. Unhappily, he died one year after his royal master, King James.

The preacher is evident in all of Purchas' works. While he was busy with the labor of compilation, he took time out to write a moral treatise which he confusingly called

Purchas his Pilgrim. Microcosmus, Or The Historie Of Man (1619), a tedious description of the genus homo, his origins, degeneration, and hope of salvation. Pious ruminations are interspersed throughout his geographical narratives and descriptions. But this very quality helped to give his writings authority and to make them interesting to his generation. Indeed, not only did the contemplation of the religions of the heathen account for the genesis of Purchas' own curiosity about the New World, but his observations concerning religion and the religious purposes which he advocated in print gained respectful and sympathetic attention from his readers. Our own failure to understand the seventeenth-century appetite for religious matter has obscured the importance of Purchas as a propagandist. After the labors of the two preachers, Hakluyt and Purchas, travel literature occupied an exalted position, which it would never have attained had it been left entirely to lay publicists or to tellers of tall tales. These clergymen found in geographical and travel literature material used in preaching a religious and patriotic crusade—a crusade which had for its objectives the extension of the benefits of Protestant religion and an expansion of the realm of England.

CHAPTER SIX

The Preachers' Plea
for Newfoundland

FOR reasons not immediately obvious today, Englishmen of the seventeenth century stubbornly clung to the notion that the north parts of America were an ambrosial paradise with a climate more benign than England's and a diversity of products that would have shamed the Indies. The coast of Maine, for example, was reputed to be rich in spices, especially cinnamon and cloves. Dates, figs, and other semitropical fruits were said to flourish with the minimum of human exertion. Vast spaces were empty Edens waiting to be settled. Furthermore, thanks to the voyages of the Cabots and other explorers later sent from England, Englishmen insisted that their title to the northern latitudes was clearer than the claim of other Europeans. Since King James was more anxious to appease than offend his enemies, the virtue of a clear title was an important argument when a Jacobean proposed settlements in North America. The good report of the country and the belief that Englishmen could settle there without becoming involved in a war with Spain, France, or Holland combined, therefore, to create renewed interest, in the late years of King James's reign, in what is now New England, Nova Scotia, and Newfoundland.

This interest focused particularly on Newfoundland, in many respects the least hospitable locality in the entire region. From the August day in 1583 when Sir Humphrey Gilbert with turf and twig had taken possession in St. John's harbor, Newfoundland had been the object of many hopeful schemes for settlement. Businessmen, appraising the rich harvest of fish from the Banks, realized that the island was a profitable asset to a maritime nation. The value of the cod dried on Newfoundland's beaches each summer was estimated at many thousands of pounds sterling. London and Bristol merchants argued stoutly that England should establish a powerful base there and police the neighboring seas, which had too often been a prey to pirates. Since the island lay athwart the route from England to the north coast of the American continent, where other colonies were projected, foreign powers must be prevented from gaining control. Profit and patriotism dictated that Newfoundland be quickly settled by sturdy Englishmen, who could neutralize the influence of Spanish, Portuguese, French, and Dutch fishermen without stirring up too many international complications.

By the end of James's reign, more than six colonies had made an effort to establish themselves on Newfoundland,[1] several writers had spent their best efforts in praising the island, and the King, the Privy Council, the Archbishops of Canterbury and York, and the clergy of all England had bestirred themselves to commend its colonization to the prayerful attention of the public.

If ever a region needed the prayers and support of godly folk, Newfoundland did, for it had become the haunt of sea rovers and a haven for the toughest fishermen that western Europe produced. It had also attracted the attention of several promoters who hoped to make money by settling plantations there, and it had drawn to its shores a motley group of ne'er-do-wells, eccentrics, hopeful working people seeking better conditions—principally from Wales, Scotland, and the west of England—and a few earnest religious souls, including Puritans, Anglicans, and Catholics.

Sir Francis Bacon had been interested in a colony, and in 1610 he and forty-six others had obtained a patent for a large tract in Newfoundland. Under the governorship of Alderman John Guy of Bristol, called "the first Christian that planted and wintered in that island," [2] a tiny settlement was immediately established. After six years Guy came home and was succeeded by Captain John Mason, who wrote a cheerful little pamphlet entitled *A Briefe Discourse of the New-found-land* (1620), which was published in Edinburgh and convinced many Scots that the island was a warmer and pleasanter spot than the homeland.

The interests of settlers and fishermen naturally clashed, and in 1615 Richard Whitbourne, a Devonshire ship captain, received an appointment as commissioner to inquire into the troubles. Already familiar with Newfoundland through many years of fishing off its shores, he added to his experience, and, like Mason, set forth his optimistic views of the island in *A Discourse And Discovery Of New-Found-Land, With many reasons to prooue how worthy and beneficiall a Plantation may there be made, after a far better manner than now it is* (1620). His treatise also exposed "Certaine Enormities and abuses committed by some that trade to that Country, and the meanes laide downe for reformation thereof." Whitbourne's book had been published by order of the Privy Council, which now enjoined the Archbishops of Canterbury and York to see that it was distributed through all the parishes of England.[3] Incidentally, two members of the Council, Lord Falkland and Sir George Calvert, were at that moment busily promoting colonies in Newfoundland. Not only were the archbishops asked to see that the book was distributed, but they were also requested to procure voluntary contributions to help reimburse Whitbourne for expenses incurred. This collection, the Privy Council thought, would be "a good encouragement to others in the like endeavours for the service of their countrie." The sending of the book to all parts of the kingdom was desirable, the Privy Council also asserted, "for the furtherance and advancement of the said plantation and to give encouragement to such as shalbe willing to adventure therein and assist the same either in their persons or otherwise, to which wee thinke the publication of his booke may much conduce." Copies of the second edition of Whitbourne's *Discourse* (1622) contain several additional documents which further disclose the activity of the civil and ecclesiastical authorities in the promotion of colonization in Newfoundland.

Immediately following the title-page of the Church

copy, preserved in the Huntington Library, is a sheet bearing on one side a proclamation from the King, dated from Theobalds, April 12, 1622, giving Whitbourne the sole right, for twenty-one years, to print his book. The proclamation also reminds the Archbishops of Canterbury and York of the desirability of publicizing the book throughout England and urges the collection of funds for the author. The King points out that the *Discourse* will be an "incouragement of Aduenturers vnto the Plantation there." On the verso of the proclamation is printed the original letter of the Privy Council to the archbishops. Tipped in as the last leaf in this book is a printed letter from George Montaigne, Bishop of London, dated September 16, 1622, instructing all the clergy throughout his diocese to do everything in their power to promote the colony and advertise Whitbourne's book. Other bishops doubtless issued similar pastoral letters.

The Bishop of London's instructions are a clear proof of the way in which the clergy were enlisted in the cause of colonial propaganda. Every ecclesiastical official, from archdeacons and deans to the lowliest of curates, was expected to give particular attention to the advertisement of Whitbourne's tract because "the publication of the said Discourse tends principally to the aduancement of his Maiesties Plantation already there begun, by inciting Aduenturers thereunto, as well as for the propagation of the Gospell in that Countrey, as also for many great benefits that may be there gotten to all such as will be Aduenturers therein; and likewise for the generall good and inriching of the whole Kingdome, . . . as by the Discourse it selfe,

herewith sent vnto you, doth more at large appeare." A
collection of funds is needed for "the Printing and free
distributing [of] his Bookes." Therefore the Bishop of
London commands the clergy to "signifie vnto your Parishioners in so friendly and effectuall manner as possibly
you can, vpon some Sabbath day, in the time of Diuine
Seruice, and when no other Collection is to be made, this
my Letter, and the scope and intent of his Discourse, and
seriously to stir vp and exhort them to extend their bounti-
full liberality herein." The churchwardens were instructed,
after the exhortation by the minister, to take up a collection and to forward the money "vnto Mr. Robert Christian, Gent. at his house in Knight-rider-street, neere the
Cathedrall Church of S. Paul in London." [4]

The commendation of Whitbourne's book, the explanation of the value of colonies in Newfoundland, and the collection must have made an impression throughout the
kingdom. If the parishioners gave heed to the volume
which they were asked to subsidize, they learned that Newfoundland was not only a profitable investment, but was
also necessary as "the meanes for increase of Defence and
Power" of England. They learned, too, that the island was
"large, temperate and fruitefull," and that the seas were
so rich that they were able to "aduance a great Trade of
Fishing, which, with Gods blessing, will become very
seruiceable to the Nauie." Colonization of the island, furthermore, would add dominions to the crown, bring glory
to the nation, and "be an aduancement of the honour of
God, in bringing poore Infidels (the Natiues of that Countrey) to his Worship, and their owne salvation." [5] Surely,

with all of these good reasons, both parson and parishioner must have felt an enthusiasm for Whitbourne and his enterprise.

Lest appeals to piety and patriotism should be insufficient to stir up interest, the worthy captain supplied other matter. In some copies of the 1620 edition, and in later editions, he appends "A conclusion to the Reader" describing a sea creature of wondrous proportions which he saw in the year 1610 by the seaside at St. John's harbor. The creature, which tried to climb into several boats, was seen by many sailors. "This (I suppose) was a Maremaid, or Mareman," he explains. "Now because diuers have writ much of Maremaids, I haue presumed to relate what is most certaine of such a strange Creature that was thus there seene, [but] whether it were a Maremaid or no, I leaue it for others to iudge." [6]

Thanks to the persuasions of the clergy, aided and abetted, perhaps, by the lure of mermaids, projects for colonizing Newfoundland, as well as the neighboring mainland, multiplied in the years immediately following the first publication of Whitbourne's *Discourse*. Whitbourne himself had commanded the second installment of colonists subsidized by Sir William Vaughan, a somewhat eccentric Welshman who wrote poetry and religious meditations. In 1621 Sir George Calvert sent out a little group, made up in part of Catholics. A year or two later, Henry Cary, Lord Falkland, bought a strip of Newfoundland and sought to settle colonists there. He also had a promotion tract published in Dublin and tried to enlist Irish emigrants. In 1622 Sir William Alexander, later Earl of

Stirling, recruited a colony of Scots and dispatched them to Nova Scotia, but they wintered in Newfoundland. In addition, he laid plans for a colony in Newfoundland, but it never materialized.[7] Meanwhile, the Pilgrims from Leyden had established themselves at Plymouth Bay. Although many of the projects for colonization came to naught, interest in the northern region simmered to a boil.

Sir William Alexander, classical scholar, poet, and dramatist, published in 1624 a tractate, entitled *An Encouragement To Colonies,* which utilized the same pious arguments set forth by the clergy. As a classicist, he, like many of the preachers, drew precedents for colonization and imperial expansion from antiquity, particularly from Roman history. Colonies, he says in a dedication to Prince Charles, will make the gospel known in foreign parts, supply necessities to many people, increase lawful commerce, and procure "glorie vnto God, honour to yourselfe, and benefit to the World." He also insisted that English colonies in America, settled on lands practically barren of other people—if a handful of savages be excepted— would approach the purity of the first age of the world, when God commanded men to go forth into the earth and multiply.[8]

Discussion of the theory and practice of colonial expansion reached a climax in 1624 with the publication of the most detailed argument for imperialism that had yet appeared. The treatise, bearing the title of *A Plaine Path-Way To Plantations,* was the work of Richard Eburne, vicar of the parish church of Henstridge, in the county of Somerset. Probably because of the rarity of the work—

only three copies are known—Eburne's reasoned treatise on the purposes and benefits of English colonies in the New World has been completely overlooked by students of British imperialism.

The Somerset parson's discussion reads like an amplification of some of the arguments suggested in Sir William Alexander's treatise, but there is no indication of collaboration. The author had, however, assimilated Whitbourne's *Discourse,* and pride in a west-country enterprise clearly stirred him to commend the development of Newfoundland. Since Bristol merchants and sailors were vitally concerned with the establishment of strong bases there, Eburne was speaking for his compatriots when he used all his powers of persuasion to convince his king and countrymen of the value of that island and the lands adjacent. Perhaps Eburne had also been moved by a suggestion from his ecclesiastical superior, the Bishop of Bath and Wells, who must have sent out a letter similar to the Bishop of London's in commendation of Whitbourne's book. In any case, Eburne dedicated his treatise to Arthur Lake, Bishop of Bath and Wells, and Robert Wright, Bishop of Bristol, to whom he wished "all health and happinesse externall, internall and eternall." Certainly these two dignitaries could not have been otherwise than pleased by Eburne's cogent reasoning in behalf of a project which the west of England heartily favored. Significantly also, Part II of the treatise has a separate dedication to Sir George Calvert, member of the Privy Council and promoter of a colony in Newfoundland. In short, the book appears to have been written, if not at the behest, at least with the tacit approval of highly placed persons directly interested in schemes to settle the New World.

The subtitle outlines the scope and objectives of the volume, describing it as "A Discourse in generall, concerning the Plantation of our English people in other Countries. Wherein Is declared, That the Attempts or Actions, in themselues are very good and laudable, necessary also for our Country of England. Doubts thereabout are answered: and some meanes are shewed, by which the same may, in better sort then hitherto, be prosecuted and effected. Written For the perswading and stirring vp of the people of this Land, chiefly the poorer and common sort to affect and effect these Attempts better then yet they doe. With certaine Motiues for a present Plantation in New-found land aboue the rest. Made in the manner of a Conference, and diuided into three Parts, for the more plainnesse, ease, and delight to the Reader.".The "conference" takes the form of a dialogue, between a farmer and a merchant, in which the merits of colonies are debated with a remarkable show of learning and wisdom, but with such clarity that, as the author intended, the simplest reader could understand.

The dedication announces that the author is writing to aid the poor and distressed of England, which had previously supported its people in prosperity but now suffers a depression. Eburne is here talking about the severe restriction in trade and consequent hardships which occurred between the years 1619 and 1624. After an era of peace and prosperity which had seen an overstimulation of credit, with resultant speculation, the financial interests of London had constricted credit.[9] A severe depression followed, and, although its causes were not clear to contemporaries, many writers, particularly among the clergy, had suggestions for its alleviation. The most popular remedy proposed was colonization abroad, and Eburne sets forth reasons to show how expansion overseas will bring a return of prosperity.

In a preface addressed to the common people of England, he asserts his desire to help his fellow countrymen by introducing them to what he calls the whole doctrine of plantations—in reality a statement of imperialistic purpose. To answer possible criticism because a preacher ventures to deal with such matters, Eburne reminds his readers that clergymen have been very forward in these affairs. He cites the instances of Master Hakluyt's great volumes of voyages, Master Crashaw's writings in behalf of colonies, and Master Whitaker's eyewitness account of the Virginia enterprise. Furthermore, if new settlements are to prosper, they must have the aid of the clergy. Indeed, the one proper and principal end of plantations should be the enlargement of Christ's church on earth and the publication of the gospel abroad. Since colonies will help the poor and advance the church, they rightfully fall within the province of the clergy.

Eburne is almost lyrical in his patriotic fervor as he reminds prospective colonists that they will carry a little of England with them wherever they go. Each new settlement will become a part of the English domain. There is no virtue in clinging to a native heath simply because one was born there. Proud and courageous men who love their country should not hover over their old hearthstones if they can benefit themselves and the state by establishing new homes overseas. In words prophetic of Rupert Brooke, Eburne urges colonists to "imagine all that to bee England where English men, where English people, you with them, and they with you, doe dwell. (And it be the people that makes the Land English, not the Land the people.) So you may finde England, and an happy England too, where now is, as I may say, no Land." [10]

The solution of England's economic difficulties lies in the establishment of new dominions abroad, where the individual, hard-pressed by poverty at home, can find ample lands and profitable opportunities. Englishmen, too numerous for lands at home to yield them adequate support, must have living room, for "Englishmen aboue many others are worst able to liue with a little." [11]

Although England needs space, Eburne does not condone ruthless aggression and seizure of territory by armed might. But, like others who debated the question of whether savages had the right to exclude settlers from thinly populated areas, he asserts that justice and Christian purpose require civilized people to occupy such lands in the New World. Where American regions are already in the possession of native populations, settlements of Englishmen may be made by declaring a protective custody over the people and giving them the benefits of civilized life in return. This form of colonization he calls planting "by Composition." Vacant areas may be settled by what he terms "Preoccupation." To the simple countryman in the dialogue, Eburne explains these policies: "We plant by *Composition*, when seeking to gaine a Country already

145

somewhat peopled and resonably inhabited, as is Guiana, we doe vpon faire conditions, as by profering them defence against their enemies, supply of their wants, namely Apparell, Armour, Edge-tooles, and the like, allure and winne them to enter league with vs, to agree that we shall dwell among them, and haue Lands and other Commodities to our content. We plant by *Preoccupation,* when finding a Country quite void of people, as no doubt in America yet there are many, as was the Barmudas, now called Summer Ilands, for [a] few yeeres past, and as is at this present, for the most part, New-found land, we seize vpon it, take it, possesse it, and as by the Lawes of God and Nations, lawfully we may hold it as our owne, and so fill and replenish it with our people." [12] He is opposed to the occupation of countries by invasion, on both moral and prudential grounds. He cannot be persuaded that it is lawful for one nation to fight against and destroy another "vpon no better title then the desire of their lands and goods." [13]

Fortunately, most of North America, particularly Newfoundland, says Eburne, is open country waiting for settlers. The few natives to be found there will profit by the exchange of lands for Christianity and civilization. Moreover, since warlike natives will not impede the settlement of Newfoundland, colonists may hope to prosper with the minimum waste of energy in defense. Aside from moral considerations, Eburne points out the immense economy of settling relatively uninhabited territory rather than trying to displace well-established and well-armed people. North America, he thinks, is ideal for occupation by law-abiding

English citizens who want prosperity rather than military glory.

An advance over most writers of the day is illustrated by Eburne's contention that the royal government should assume the responsibility for colonial expansion rather than leave settlements abroad to the hazards of chance, or private investment. His advocacy of colonization by government instead of private stock company perhaps is a reflection of King James's current feud with the Virginia Company, which resulted in the revocation of its charter in 1624. At any rate, Eburne presents logical arguments in favor of government initiative in colonial enterprise. "His Maiestie would be pleased to entitle himselfe King and supreme Gouernour of that Countrey, wherein the Plantation shall proceed, as at this present of New-found-Land," he declares, "that so they that plant and dwell there, may know directly and expressly vnder whose dominions they dwell." Many people would be induced to settle in colonies abroad if they could be certain of remaining within the dominions of England. Although the interlocutor in the dialogue observes that the royal prerogative is made manifest in the letters patent issued to all private companies, the expositor declares that the King's authority over colonies ought to be proclaimed in every town and city of England. Furthermore, "if in euerie Church, he [the King] were prayed for by the Name of King of that Countrey, as well as of England, France, and Ireland," [14] the nation would come to realize the new extent of his dominions. The King's assumption of rule would not discourage individual enterprise—which Eburne thinks should be fostered—but would make English settlers in a new land citizens of an empire instead of mere participants in a private undertaking.

Eburne is consciously an imperialist. Here and there throughout the treatise he cites examples of Roman precedent in colonial policy and holds up imperial Rome as worthy of emulation.

In addition to presenting the "doctrine of plantations"— the theory of expansion—Eburne gives much practical advice for both promoters and colonists. He suggests more effective propaganda in order to arouse the public to a greater zeal for settlement overseas; he urges an adequate supply of ministers to care for the needs of settlers and preach the gospel to the heathen; he recommends nine ways of raising funds for colonial activities—including lotteries and the use of money donated to the church. To answer the criticism that emigrants would exhaust the country by taking out too much money, he advocates a managed currency for circulation in the colonies; and he urges that industrious craftsmen and artisans be given preference as emigrants. Particularly, he warns against handicapping a new colony with shiftless idlers. Evidently Master Eburne had conferred with returned travelers from Virginia and knew some of the mistakes of the earlier venture.

Idleness he regards as the great sin of England—idleness and the love of ease. The hardships of frontier life he believes will restore the nation to its former strength and prowess. That benefit alone would justify all the money and effort spent in establishing colonies abroad, for the seeds of ruin are already evident in the softness of Englishmen. "We must not greatly maruell," Eburne remarks, "if our so long continued rest and peace from warres and war-like imployments, our vnspeakable idleness and dissolute life, haue so corrupted and in manner effeminated our people generally and for the most part, that they cannot endure the hearing, much lesse the doing of any laborious attempts, of any thing that shall be troublous or any whit dangerous vnto them." [15] The remedy for such weakness will be found in the labor of colonizing a new country, and to this end he prays that an act of Parliament might be passed to bring such enterprises under "Regall and Legall authoritie," for they cannot be accomplished "by priuate agreements and directions only."

Richard Eburne's tractate is a sermon on the national welfare. Its main purpose is to arouse the plain people of England to a realization of the opportunities beckoning to them from beyond the seas. But the author also hopes that king and Parliament will listen to the wisdom with which the merchant in the dialogue instructs the simple farmer. An empire is at stake. And England must not be allowed to sleep. If Eburne persuaded no one else, he at least convinced himself, for at the close of the book he prints in the margin: "The Author himselfe doth purpose God willing to goe into one or other Plantation."

The clergy, from the Archbishop of Canterbury to the vicar of Henstridge, had raised their voices in behalf of Newfoundland. If that colony failed to prosper, it was not proof that their labor had been wasted. They had advanced the "doctrine of plantations" and had led public opinion a little further along the path of empire.

CHAPTER SEVEN

Religion and the
Sense of Destiny

WHATEVER misgivings Tudor and Stuart preachers might have had about certain problems of theology, they never lacked confidence in their ability to give proper advice in matters temporal. They were the sociologists of the day. Their sermons, as we have seen, were often tractates on subjects quite mundane, albeit vital to the citizen and the state. Their professional duty required them to take cognizance of all questions of human behavior, as well as problems of economics and politics—insofar as they dared. The pulpit was a forum, and the preacher was both a teacher and a leader. Since the clergy were among the most articulate and vocal members of society, they not only gave expression to ideas that were current, but they also helped to shape the thought and opinion of their time. In the jargon of the present day, they were among the most alert of the "social thinkers." This quality was characteristic of the clergy without dis-

tinction of sect. Anglicans and Puritans were equally out-
spoken on social problems.

That the merits of colonial expansion should have been
advocated by all sections of the English clergy occasions no
surprise. The preachers sincerely believed that colonies
offered a solution of many of the spiritual, moral, and economic ills of England. Moreover, the preachers believed
that their countrymen, in carrying English civilization and
the Protestant religion to unbaptized infidels, would be the
instruments of the divine will. Gradually, they induced in
public consciousness a sense of mission, a feeling often not
put into words but nonetheless strong, that Englishmen
had a destiny overseas.

That promoters should have made use of the clergy to
advertise schemes for settlements overseas is equally understandable. No better medium for propaganda existed in the
sixteenth and seventeenth centuries. Lacking the facilities
of a British Broadcasting Company and a highly developed
press, the government and the stock companies utilized the
next-best thing to a loud-speaker: they induced the preachers to broadcast information and commendations of their
projects.

A close bond developed between religion and trade. By
and large, the clergy of Jacobean England were good
mercantilists. The policies they advocated were those that
appealed to the men of commerce. They believed that
poverty at home could be relieved by the development of
trade and plantations. Colonies would provide the where-
withal to augment employment of English craftsmen,

would create abroad a market for English manufactures, and would also give an outlet for the surplus population.

In expansion the preachers saw an opportunity for increasing the work available to the poor and for eliminating idleness. Seventeenth-century preachers, Anglicans and Puritans alike, looked upon idleness and consequent poverty as moral iniquities. Indeed, most of the grosser sins originated in the one sin of idleness. Hence unemployment was an evil that must be removed as much for moral as for economic reasons. The clerical attitude toward unemployment was not without its humanitarian side, to be sure, but the predominant reason for waging war against idleness was moral. As Richard Eburne so earnestly argued, plantations would provide work, and thus English character, corrupted by sloth and ease, would be restored. The gospel of work embraced in its scope the related prudential virtues of diligence, thrift, sobriety, and honesty. Trade and plantations were a sort of cure-all that appealed to preachers of various sects.

The modern cynic is likely to see something cold-bloodedly iniquitous in the close coöperation between the clergy and the commercial companies of the late sixteenth and early seventeenth centuries. Actually, most ministers and businessmen were sincerely convinced that they were carrying out a noble plan for the benefit of mankind. Nothing but good could come, they believed, from efforts to provide a means of self-help for the poor. Trading companies and colonial projects promised to relieve distress and bring honor to the nation, glory to the crown, and the extension of God's kingdom. Incidental profits to shareholders, even if they ran to two hundred per cent or more, were proof of the divine blessing upon beneficent enterprises.

The ideas advanced by the clergy in their sponsorship of trade and colonies were not, of course, entirely original with them. Although some of the preachers, steeped in the history of Rome and the classical world, were a little ahead of their time in discernment of an imperial design, most of them simply put into words notions that were in the air—notions that merchants, promoters, and statesmen had on their tongues. In fact, certain of the documents prepared by very realistic laymen sound like the arguments of preachers. For example, a letter of advice from Sir Francis Bacon to the Duke of Buckingham contains a number of the same suggestions about colonies that one finds in Richard Eburne or William Crashaw. He even urges a particular care for religion, the elimination from new plantations of all schismatics (especially elimination of Roman Catholics and Anabaptists), and a strict caution to avoid the extirpation of natives under the pretense of religion. "God," he says, "surely will no way be pleased with such sacrifices." [1] Religion was extremely important in the eyes of laymen, even of such rationalists as Francis Bacon, and they gave it a place of first importance in schemes for expansion overseas.

The great significance of the preachers' efforts for expansion lay less in the originality of their views than in the prestige which their position gave to opinions expressed from the pulpit. At few times in the history of England has the pulpit enjoyed a greater reputation than it had during the reign of James. The King himself was a connoisseur of sermons and attended preaching regularly. He and his courtiers set an example by turning out for sermons at Paul's Cross. John Chamberlain's letters to Dudley Carleton are full of reports of the King's reaction to sermons—reactions not always favorable—and of instructions directly from the court for the insertion of particular propaganda. Occasionally, the King himself suggested texts for a Paul's Cross sermon or a sermon at the court, and he frequently gave his royal opinion on points of doctrine or biblical scholarship.[2]

The royal appetite for sermons was matched by the zest with which commoners listened to the preachers and bought their published homilies. A large proportion of the output of the printing press consisted of religious books, especially sermons and handbooks of piety written by preachers. The public looked to the ministers for guidance in every detail of life.[3] How carefully laymen heeded the advice given is another question, but there can be no dispute over the quantity of counsel from the pulpit that reached every English citizen.

The specific degree of influence exerted by the clergy in behalf of foreign trade and colonial expansion cannot, of course, be measured. We can only reason that the best propagandic agency of the day, by continued advocacy of a definite program, must have carried tremendous weight in the gradual education of the citizenry to opportunities overseas.

The problem of expansion was not merely one of securing sufficient stock subscriptions and adequate governmental authority, but was also one of inculcating in enough people the desire to emigrate. Englishmen needed persuasion and reassurance. They needed to be convinced that they would better their condition and prosper in a new land. They needed the comforting suggestion that God himself would smile upon their endeavors and bless them for carrying English ways and religion to the heathen. All of these ideas preachers throughout the country constantly repeated until they became a part of Jacobean dogma. Proof of the influence of the clergy may be found in the eagerness of the trading companies and overseas promoters to secure the services and the good report of ministers.

The reasons that persuaded seventeenth-century Englishmen to colonize abroad were diverse and often mixed.[4] Economic, political, and religious motives each played a part in the settlement of America. All of these motives are reflected in the writings and utterances of Jacobean preachers.

One particular political issue the clergy kept alive. That was the danger to England from Catholic Spain. The Protestant clergy unanimously agreed that Spain must be thwarted in her colonial empire. From the reign of Elizabeth to the end of James's life, and later, the preachers waged an incessant and bitter war against Spain. Although James made a formal peace with Spain in 1604, the clergy never recognized an armistice. Occasionally, they went too far and suffered for their boldness, as when they criticized severely the proposed Spanish match of Prince Charles in 1623, but they never relaxed their vigilance to warn the public against the powers of anti-Christ, as Spain was most frequently described. With the increase of Puritanism, the attack on Spain intensified, and English Puritans on two continents continued an ideological war against Spain.[5] The campaign begun by Elizabethan and Jacobean preachers was intimately connected with their zeal for expansion overseas. The preservation of the Protestant faith and the English realm depended upon clipping the wings of the Spanish eagle. This argument cannot have failed to carry conviction to many a zealous English Protestant who may have been deaf to other pleas.

The Puritan migrations in the reign of Charles I produced another host of preachers who arose to glorify the new country and to magnify the sense of destiny. The part played by religion in the development of New England is too well known to bear repeating and is outside the scope of the present discussion, but a few facts are worth mentioning in connection with the earlier religious propaganda for expansion. The groundwork for many of the Puritans' arguments concerning God's especial care for his saints had been laid by Jacobean preachers of various degrees of conformity. For once Anglicans and Puritans found themselves sharing similar opinions about the virtues of trade and plantations and the iniquity and danger of Spain. They both believed that Englishmen would serve God and the nation by carving out new territories across the western seas. With a singleness of purpose rarely found among preachers, they took upon themselves the task of proving to their countrymen that profit and patriotism could be combined by settling plantations in America. The public was gradually convinced, and the tide of colonization had already set in by the accession of Charles I.

The intensification of the sense of divine mission developed by the Puritans who settled New England had an influence that profoundly affected, not only the internal affairs of the colonies, but also the attitude in England toward expansion—and, indeed, the later course of expansion on the American continent.

From 1630 onward, New England became a haven of refuge for nonconformists fleeing from the tyranny of Archbishop Laud and the Court of High Commission. To pious Puritans, the theocracy established in Massachusetts Bay seemed to herald the millennium, and many Puritan divines almost lyrically described the virtues of that colony, with its freedom from bishops. One "sup of New England Aire is better than a whole draft of old Englands Ale," asserted the Reverend Samuel Higginson in an ecstatic moment.[6] The pioneers of New England were convinced that they were the children of God, another Chosen People. Their sense of election operated to their material advantage and gave them a valuable assurance of right in all their endeavors. Like an Old Testament prophet, William Bradford described the victory over the Pequot Indians at Mystic fort in 1637 as a signal proof of the quality of Jehovah's wrath toward the enemies of his people: "It was a fearfull sight to see them thus frying in ye fyer," he says in telling of the burning of the Indian fort, "and ye streams of blood quenching ye same, and horrible was ye stinck & sente therof; but ye victory seemed

157

a sweete sacrifice, and they gave the prays therof to God, who had wrought so wonderfuly for them, thus to inclose their enimise in their hands, and give them so speedy a victory over so proud & insulting an enimie." [7] A traditional story, doubtless apocryphal, about the early settlers of Milford, Connecticut, further illustrates the Puritan sense of election. Finding themselves troubled in conscience about taking land from the Indians, the inhabitants in 1640 held a town meeting to discuss the problem. After surveying the Scriptures, they solemnly voted and ordered their decision inscribed in the minutes of the meeting. The syllogism which soothed their consciences read:

"1. The earth is the Lord's and the fullness thereof. Voted.

"2. The Lord can dispose of the earth to his saints. Voted.

"3. We are his saints. Voted." [8]

This feeling of being a part of a divine plan, of being especially elected of God to carry out his will as it was unfolded to them, was an emotion that we can only dimly understand today. We may smile at the materialistic application that Puritans made of religion, but that was only part of the story. They were convinced of their destiny and their mission. And the great Puritan Migration from 1630 onward was more than a mere transplantation of farmers and craftsmen. It was a vast movement that spent its force only when the luxury and ease of the nineteenth century corrupted the moral and religious forces of the Puritan people. The impact upon England of the Puritan westward movement was powerful, and its influence upon the

New World was permanent. The elected children of God were on the way, and they maintained their belief in their high destiny until the whole North American continent and lands even beyond the China Sea had felt their power. Few movements in modern history have had such a profound effect as the Puritan Migration, with all that it brought in its train. Students of American history sometimes talk of Manifest Destiny as if it had been invented by President Polk and his contemporaries. But the Puritans who moved inexorably upon the New World had a belief in Manifest Destiny that makes the later American imperialism look anemic and pale. They were the allies of God, and they fortified themselves for their task by an adherence to a stern code of prudential morality which emphasized diligence, thrift, sobriety, and care for one's credit—cornerstones of bourgeois ethics. Before the Puritans' relentless onslaught, Indians, Spaniards, Frenchmen, and all others gave way. The dream of Elizabethan and Jacobean Englishmen of a bulwark against Spain in North America was more than realized before the end of the seventeenth century—and yet the empire continued to move ever westward.

From time to time in the history of the world, religion, politics, and economics have united to create some powerful movement. The rise and spread of Mohammedanism may be explained by the force of this explosive mixture. In a lesser way, the Mormon migration illustrates the same process. In American history, the strength of evangelical Christianity, with its political and economic corollaries, has been one of the most persistent and influential forces.

The Puritan doctrines of New England gave to America some of its most unlovable qualities. Intolerance, acquisitiveness, materialism, and the suppression of the softer amenities of life found rationalization in the Puritan philosophy, but these qualities—disagreeable as they are to us—gave a Spartan strength to the pioneers of New England and helped them to survive the rigors of an inhospitable climate and the hostility of crafty Indians. These qualities, combined with an emphasis on diligence—work as an end in itself—thrift, and sobriety, created a race stern and strong enough to push across forest and desert until all the land was theirs. No man can measure the value of Puritan religion in the winning of America. We may deplore the narrowness and the residual bigotry that we have inherited from the Puritans, but as historians we must recognize the tremendous force that they provided in the conquest of the new Canaan.

British and American expansion in the Pacific likewise owed much to the influence of religion. Indeed, the foreign policies, there, of both England and the United States have been vitally affected by religious interests.

We think of Captain Cook as the man who opened the eyes of England and America to the beauties and opportunities of the South Seas, but we ought also to remember the missionaries who followed in his wake.

One of the strangest tales in the annals of British expansion is the story of the conquest of Polynesia by puritanical tradesmen of the London Missionary Society, who first landed in Tahiti on March 5, 1797, from the ship "Duff." [9] The saviors of Polynesia were the spiritual descendants of seventeenth-century Puritans. Indeed, they were Congregationalists who would have felt at home in Boston in 1650. But their imaginations had been stirred by a new stimulus: the beliefs of Rousseau in the noble savage, although none of the missionaries realized that he was under the influence of this atheistic Frenchman.

After Captain Cook's expedition to Tahiti in 1769, Dr. John Hawkesworth dressed up a narrative of Cook's and other explorations in the South Seas, and published it as *An Account of the Voyages . . . in the Southern Hemisphere . . .* (1773). Hawkesworth dwelt on the perfection of these island paradises. Strongly under the influence of Rousseau, he pictured the natives as the sum of all earthly charm and beauty. Hawkesworth's book, and other accounts even more alluring, were noised abroad, until a group of pious London shopkeepers found themselves fascinated. They read about the Tahitians and they felt a call to go to this island Macedonia, where dwelt a race of gentle and perfect people, destined to perdition simply because they had not heard the gospel message. Moved by an urgency to save them, a group of tradesmen organized the London Missionary Society and chartered the ship "Duff."

Only four of the first missionaries were ordained ministers, but the rest of the party were fired by a great missionary zeal. Some of their names will indicate the composition of the group: William Smith, linen draper; Edward Hudden, butcher; Seth Kelso, weaver; William Crook, gentleman's servant; John Buchanan, tailor; Benjamin Broomhall, harness maker; Henry Nott, bricklayer; and William Henry, carpenter. These were the vanguard who first carried the British flag to permanent settlements in Polynesia.

The two problems that chiefly disturbed the missionaries were the nudity of the Tahitians and their lack of a sense of private property. Both of these defects were quickly remedied by the energetic newcomers. They dressed the natives in the drab garb that English men and women wore in 1797, and they induced in them such a sense of private possessions that they quickly developed civilized qualities of greed. But the natives also influenced the missionaries. A few months after landing, the group leaders were disturbed by the practical question of whether it was proper for a missionary to marry a heathen woman, and decided that it was not. Whereupon one of the brethren, Benjamin Broomhall, the harness maker, decided that he no longer believed in hell and absconded with a native woman.

But, despite the softening effect of the South Seas, within a few years the stern Puritans of the London Missionary Society had extended their sway over many islands and had changed the people into as close an approach to bourgeois Englishmen as was humanly possible. To this day, the Puritanism of the first missionaries continues to rule many islands, and one can find in Polynesia perfect examples of the seventeenth-century Puritan community, with many of the blue laws familiar in colonial Boston still operative.

Spurred by missionary zeal, London Missionary Society representatives gained control of the Society Islands, the Cook group, Samoa, and many other scattered islands. On the basis of their settlements, the British government in a later period argued its claims to sovereignty.

The United States owes Hawaii to the effort of the missionaries. Although we did not formally annex the islands until 1898, they had been potentially an American domain since the arrival of a Puritan missionary delegation from New England in 1820.[10] Under the leadership of the Reverend Hiram Bingham the missionaries quickly converted the unresisting Hawaiians and soon found it expedient to acquire large holdings of the best lands. Today the first families of Hawaii trace their ancestry and their financial endowments to the Puritan zeal of the early missionaries.

The New England missionaries to Hawaii had been stirred to save the heathen there by the vivid descriptions of returning sea traders and whalers who had wintered in the tropical paradise. The missionary movement emanated from Goshen, Connecticut, where a rousing meeting was held on September 29, 1819. Significantly, the sermon ordaining the first missionaries was preached from a text in the Book of Joshua—the same chapter that had been used by Jacobean propagandists for colonization—"And there remaineth yet much land to be possessed." The preacher, the Reverend Heman Humphrey, pastor of the Congregational Church at Pittsfield, Massachusetts, reminded his audience that a new Chosen People, like the Israelites of old, were going out from the land of Goshen—this time, Goshen, Connecticut—to claim and redeem a new Canaan for Jehovah. His sermon might have been written by any of the imperialist preachers of the seventeenth century.

The American missionaries had the same code of ethics

as that of the seventeenth century, the same feeling that commerce and religion could and should be welded into a congenial fellowship. How well they succeeded is evident in the economic and social history of the Hawaiian Islands.

American foreign policy in Asia has been tremendously influenced by the popular concepts of China, Japan, and India received from missionaries. Many of us have heard the returned missionary from China relate his experiences and describe the manners and customs of the Chinese and their need for the benefits of "civilization"—our civilization—as represented by the Singer Sewing Machine Company and the products of the Standard Oil Company. The penetration of China by American interests has been vastly aided by the missionaries.

Americans have always had a sentimental interest in China, stimulated over the years by missionary reports in thousands of country churches throughout the nation. Popular opinion has been opposed to the sort of partition of China which other powers advocated. The "Open Door" policy was not dictated solely by the self-interest of American commerce. It was regarded as just and fair by simple citizens who knew China through the interpretations of the missionaries. When China paid us an indemnity after the Boxer Rebellion, we utilized the money to found scholarships, in American colleges and universities, for Chinese students. China has always been a favorite of Americans—a favorite cultivated by the endeavors of thousands of missionaries sent out by a score of American sects and denominations. At the present moment, that long propaganda is paying off an unforeseen dividend.

To the twentieth century, the motives and purposes of the religious groups who so powerfully affected the expansion of English-speaking peoples may seem narrow and hypocritical. But that interpretation ignores the spirit of the times which produced the movements that we have been discussing. Self-interest there certainly was. But to doubt the sincerity of these people is to misunderstand the age in which they lived. Once more let me emphasize that they were conscious of being a part of a great undertaking, of being the instruments of God's will, and, if profits accrued to them, it was a clear indication of the favor of the Almighty. The Hebraic, Old Testament faith of the men and women of the seventeenth century and of their spiritual descendants in later periods was often harsh and conducive to bigotry. But it had sinews and strength.

Today we smile in a superior fashion at the naïveté of their religion and the way it was used as the handmaiden of self-interest. But we ought to ask ourselves what we have put in its place. The totalitarian dictators have taunted us with our moral and spiritual flabbiness, and their jibes have touched a weak spot in our national character. Although no worshiper of the past would wish a return of seventeenth-century Puritanism, and no sensible person would be fooled by the mystical rigmarole of the Nazi creed, many Americans have felt that the lack of a positive national faith and goal has been one of our greatest shortcomings. Historically, we must be aware that a nation without a zeal for something besides its own ease and comfort is doomed. Ironically, the war has supplied a crusading purpose, and when the war is won we shall have a tremendous role thrust upon us. We can no longer be content with getting and spending. We shall have to assume international responsibilities that we have long shirked. We may substitute for the religious and expansionist zeal of the seventeenth century a passion for true patriotism. We may return to the Renaissance concept of service to the state as the highest purpose of man in society. Without doubt, reshaping the state and remaking the world will require the best brains that we can produce; the alternative is to drift into chaos.

America unwillingly has had international expansion thrust upon it. We may hope that it will not assume the character of older types of imperialism. When the war is over, we may have to assume the leadership of the fragments of the English-speaking world. We cannot escape this destiny if we win. We no longer have the religion of our seventeenth-century forbears to give us a sense of divine mission, but we must develop a rational belief in our obligations and responsibilities. No fine altruistic verbiage need concern us. We want to survive, and we want democratic institutions to live. Unless we develop a belief in ourselves and an almost fanatical faith in our destiny, we shall continue to sleepwalk on the brink of ruin. A new cycle of expansion has overtaken us, and we shall need all the residual strength and inner force of our seventeenth-century ancestors if we are to fulfill our mission.

NOTES

INDEX

Notes

CHAPTER I

1. Sir C. Alexander Harris (ed.), *A Relation of a Voyage to Guiana by Robert Harcourt, 1613* (Hakluyt Society, 2d Ser., LX; London, 1926), p. 31.

2. James A. Williamson, *A Short History of British Expansion: The Old Colonial Empire* (London, 1930), pp. 157–58. For a brief discussion on the other side of the question, see Sir Charles Lucas, *Religion, Colonizing, and Trade: Driving Forces of the Old Empire* (London, 1930), pp. 1–35.

For other sidelights on the motives of early English expansionists, see also James A. Williamson, *The Ocean in English History* (Oxford, 1941)—a volume which the present writer did not have an opportunity of reading until his own work was completed.

3. Sir Walter Raleigh, "The English Voyages of the Sixteenth Century," in an essay in the index volume of Richard Hakluyt's *The Principal Navigations* (XII [Glasgow, 1905]), pp. 13–14. See also, Samuel Eliot Morison, *Admiral of the Ocean Sea: A Life of Christopher Columbus* (Boston, 1942), *passim*.

4. Samuel Purchas, *Hakluytus Posthumus, or, Purchas His Pilgrimes*, XIX (Glasgow, 1906), 480.

5. Hakluyt, *Principal Navigations*, VIII, 2.

6. *Ibid.*, II, 199.

7. William S. Page, *The Russia Company from 1553 to 1660* (London, n.d.), p. 6.

8. Clements R. Markham (ed.), *The Hawkins' Voyages during the Reigns of Henry VIII, Queen Elizabeth, and James I* (Hakluyt Society, LVII; London, 1878), p. 9. Further evidence of pious

observances on Sir John Hawkins' voyages was given in the testimony of some of his captured seamen before the Inquisition in Mexico. See Frank Aydelotte, "Elizabethan Seamen in Mexico and Ports of the Spanish Main," *The American Historical Review*, XLVIII (1942), 1–19.

9. Markham, *op. cit.*, p. 25. The account of the voyage, quoted here, was written by John Sparke the younger, who went on the voyage.

10. *Ibid.*, p. xv. Quoted by Markham.

11. G. P., *A True Reporte, Of the late discoueries, . . . by that valiaunt and worthye Gentleman, Sir Humfrey Gilbert Knight* (1583), prefatory poem signed by John Hawkins.

12. Reprinted by Markham, *op. cit.*, pp. 83–329. See pp. 90, 93, 126, 185–86, 209–10.

13. Richard Collinson (ed.), *The Three Voyages of Martin Frobisher in Search of a Passage to Cathaia and India by the North-West, A.D. 1576–8* (Hakluyt Society, XXXVIII; London, 1868), p. 20. Best's account is entitled *A True Discourse Of The Late Voyages Of Discouerie For Finding Of A Passage To Cathaya, By The North-Weast, Under The Conduct of Martin Frobisher General* (1578).

14. *Ibid.*, p. 128.

15. *Ibid.*, p. 217.

16. James R. Dasent (ed.), *Acts of the Privy Council, . . . 1577–1578* (London, 1895), p. 213.

17. Collinson (ed.), *op. cit.*, p. 229.

18. *Ibid.*, pp. 238, 246–47.

19. *Ibid.*, p. 230. See also pp. 272–73.

20. *Ibid.*, p. 252.

21. Julian S. Corbett, *Drake and the Tudor Navy* (London, 1898), I, 66–68.

22. *Ibid.*, pp. 259–60. See also W. S. W. Vaux (ed.), *The World Encompassed by Sir Francis Drake* (Hakluyt Society, XVI; London, 1854), p. 67. This narrative was compiled and first published in

1628, principally from notes kept by Francis Fletcher. Vaux, however, adds other important documents in appendixes.

23. Corbett, *op. cit.*, I, 262.

24. Vaux (ed.), *op. cit.*, p. 71.

25. *Ibid.*, p. 81.

26. *Ibid.*, p. 114.

27. *Ibid.*, p. 124.

28. *Ibid.*, pp. 151–56.

29. Hakluyt, *Principal Navigations*, XI, 114.

30. Vaux, *op. cit.*, appendix, p. 176. For a full account of this episode, see Corbett, *op. cit.*, I, 320–22.

31. A popular account of Madox' career, as well as some information about John Walker, with particular references to this voyage, may be found in George Walker, *Puritan Salt: The Story of Richard Madox, Elizabethan Venturer* (London, 1935).

32. Hakluyt, *Principal Navigations*, XI, 170–71.

33. Walker, *op. cit.*, p. 50.

34. *Ibid.*, pp. 97–119, where the sermon is reprinted.

35. *Ibid.*, p. 165.

36. *Ibid.*, p. 166.

37. *Ibid.*, p. 177.

38. Hakluyt, *Principal Navigations*, XI, 184.

39. Williamson, *Short History of British Expansion*, pp. 129–30. For pertinent documents concerning Gilbert's career, see Carlos Slafter (ed.), *Sir Humfrey Gylberte and His Enterprise of Colonization in America* (The Prince Society, XXIX; Boston, 1903), *passim*, and David B. Quinn (ed.), *The Voyages and Colonising Enterprises of Sir Humphrey Gilbert* (Hakluyt Society, 2d Ser., LXXXIII–LXXXIV; London, 1940).

40. Hakluyt, *Principal Navigations*, VIII, 74.

41. *Ibid.*, p. 36.

42. *Ibid.*, p. 38.

43. *Ibid.*, p. 72.

44. See George B. Parks, "George Peele and His Friends as

'Ghost'-Poets," *Journal of English and Germanic Philology*, XLI (1942), 527–36. Professor Parks suggests that G. P., generally believed to stand for Sir George Peckham, one of the backers of Gilbert's expedition, was instead George Peele, the poet.

45. Ed. of 1583, sig. B3 verso.

46. Albert H. Markham (ed.), *The Voyages and Works of John Davis, the Navigator* (Hakluyt Society, LIX; London, 1880), pp. 114–15.

47. *Ibid.*, p. 112.

48. *Ibid.*, p. 224.

49. *Ibid.*, p. 228.

50. *Ibid.*, p. 236. The earliest extant edition of the *The Seamans Secrets* is that of 1607, but the book was recorded in the *Stationers' Register* on September 3, 1594.

51. James Orchard Halliwell (ed.), *The Private Diary of Dr. John Dee* (Camden Society, XIX; London, 1842), p. 18. Entries for January 23, 24, 1583.

52. Sir Robert H. Schomburgk (ed.), *The Discovery of the Large, Rich, and Beautiful Empire of Guiana . . . by Sir Walter Ralegh, Knt.* (Hakluyt Society, III; London, 1848), p. 135. The manuscript from which this quotation is taken is preserved among the Sloane MSS, 1133, fol. 45. It was apparently written soon after the first voyage to Guiana, probably about 1596.

53. *Ibid.*, p. 140.

54. *Ibid.*, p. 143.

55. Purchas, *Pilgrimes*, XVI, 44–45.

56. Edward P. Cheyney, *A History of England from the Defeat of the Armada to the Death of Elizabeth* (London, 1926), II, 58. The prayer attributed to Queen Elizabeth is to be found in Hakluyt, *Principal Navigations*, IV, 239–40.

57. Purchas, *Pilgrimes*, XIV, 306 ff. See also Henry Stevens (ed.), *The Dawn of British Trade to the East Indies as Recorded in the Court Minutes of the East India Company, 1599–1603* (London, 1886), pp. 216, 228, 232.

CHAPTER II

1. The biography of Richard Hakluyt has been ably treated by Professor George Parks in *Richard Hakluyt and the English Voyages* (New York, 1928). Anyone who now writes about Hakluyt must stand in Professor Parks's debt, and I am particularly under obligation to him. Sir Walter Raleigh's "The English Voyages of the Sixteenth Century," in the MacLehose edition of Hakluyt's *The Principal Navigations* (Glasgow, 1905), XII, is provocative. Useful also is the introduction to E. G. R. Taylor (ed.), *The Original Writings and Correspondence of the Two Richard Hakluyts* (The Hakluyt Society, 2d Ser., LXXVI; London, 1935).

2. Reprinted in Taylor (ed.), *Original Writings*, II, 396–97.

3. *Ibid.*, p. 397.

4. *Ibid.*

5. Barlow was also the author of a useful treatise on terrestrial magnetism and the properties of the loadstone, entitled *Magneticall Aduertisements* (1616). In a dedication to Sir Dudley Digges, he praises the merchants and gentlemen who have supported "discoueries of vnknown passages to new Countries and Nations, for the further aduancement of Gods glorie, the honour of our King, and principall benefit of the whole Kingdome."

6. The main facts of Hakluyt's career are easily followed in the "annals" provided by Professor Parks, *op. cit.*, pp. 242–59.

7. *Ibid.*, pp. 201–2.

8. Taylor (ed.), *Original Writings*, I, 139–46.

9. *Ibid.*, II, 211–326. See also the comment by Parks, *op. cit.*, pp. 87–98. Hakluyt apparently regarded this paper as too bold to warrant its publication.

10. Taylor (ed.), *Original Writings*, II, 215.

11. *Ibid.*, p. 245.

12. *Ibid.*, pp. 313–19.

13. *Ibid.*, pp. 324–25.

14. *Ibid.*, p. 326.

15. *Ibid.*, p. 376.

16. René de Laudonnière, *A Notable Historie containing foure voyages made by certayne French Captaynes vnto Florida* (1587), sig. Q4 verso.

17. Parks, *op. cit.*, pp. 250–51.

18. Taylor (ed.), *Original Writings*, II, 400.

19. *Ibid.*, p. 457.

20. *Ibid.*, p. 462.

21. Parks, *op. cit.*, p. 256.

22. *Ibid.*, p. 257.

23. For a further note on his activities for the Virginia Company, see below, chap. IV, note 1.

24. Parks, *op. cit.*, p. 212.

25. Taylor (ed.), *Original Writings*, II, 420–25. These two papers are also reprinted in Alexander Brown, *The Genesis of the United States* (London, 1890), II, 669–75.

CHAPTER III

1. For a work assembling with admirable documentation the evidence of English interest in the Near East, see Samuel C. Chew, *The Crescent and the Rose: Islam and England during the Renaissance* (New York, 1937). The influence of voyages to the East, and elsewhere, upon Elizabethan men of letters is described in two books by Robert R. Cawley: *Unpathed Waters: Studies in the Influence of the Voyagers on Elizabethan Literature* (Princeton, 1940) and *The Voyagers and Elizabethan Drama* (Modern Language Association Monograph Series; Boston, 1938).

2. William Samuel Page, *The Russia Company from 1553 to 1660* (London, n.d.), p. 87.

3. Alfred C. Wood, *A History of the Levant Company* (Oxford, 1935), pp. 222–24. I have been unable to see J. B. Pearson, *Biographical Sketches of the Chaplains to the Levant Company, 1611–*

1706 (Cambridge, 1883). Apparently no copy is available in the United States, and a photographic reproduction has been unobtainable from England.

4. For an account of this episode, see Chew, *op. cit.*, p. 162.

5. Henry Stevens (ed.), *The Dawn of British Trade to the East Indies as Recorded in the Court Minutes of the East India Company, 1599–1603* (London, 1886), pp. 275–76. The writer of the letter, which is dated March, 1599/1600, is not given, but the context makes it clear that Smith was the author. In the quotation cited here, contractions have been expanded.

6. Samuel Purchas, *Hakluytus Posthumus, or, Purchas His Pilgrimes*, VIII (Glasgow, 1905), 248–304.

7. The identity of the chaplain of Aleppo and the factor of Surat as one and the same person cannot be stated as a certainty, but from hints in the letters it seems clear that they were the same. See William Foster (ed.), *Letters Received by the East India Company from Its Servants in the East* (London, 1897), II, 134 *et passim*.

8. Chew, *op. cit.*, p. 46.

9. Robson, *Newes From Aleppo*, p. 14.

10. Foster (ed.), *Letters*, VI, xxxix.

11. *Calendar of State Papers, Colonial Series, East Indies, China and Japan, 1513–1616* (London, 1862), pp. 182, 286. The court minutes of the East India Company, calendared in the State Papers of this and succeeding series, contain references to an incredible amount of official attention to chaplains and religious problems.

12. *Ibid.*, pp. 285, 291.

13. Foster (ed.), *Letters*, VI, 193–94.

14. *Cal. S. P., Col., East Indies, 1513–1616*, p. 330.

15. *Ibid.*, *1617–1621*, p. 249.

16. Foster (ed.), *Letters*, III, 76–77.

17. *Ibid.*, p. 92.

18. Clements R. Markham (ed.), *The Voyages of Sir James Lancaster, Kt., to the East Indies* (Hakluyt Society, 1st Ser., LVI; London, 1877), pp. 228–29.

19. *Ibid.*, pp. 234–35. For evidence that the religious instruction

ordered on this voyage, and the piety displayed on the "Hoseander," were characteristic of the East Indian voyages of this period, see Sir George Birdwood and Sir William Foster (eds.), *The Register of Letters, &c. of the Governour and Company of Merchants of London Trading into the East Indies, 1600–1619* (London, 1893), pp. 53, 116, 241, 296, 322–23, 329–30, 370, 397, *et passim*.

20. Birdwood and Foster (eds.), *Register*, p. 419. See also p. 397. Cf. *Cal. S. P., Col., East Indies, 1513–1616*, p. 183, recording an order of the company to provide a ship with a Bible, Foxe's *Book of Martyrs*, and "some good book of sermons." Scattered through the court minutes are similar evidences of the company's desire to keep the ships supplied with religious books.

21. Maunde Thompson (ed.), *Diary of Richard Cocks, Cape-Merchant in the English Factory in Japan, 1615–1622* (Hakluyt Society, 1st Ser., LXVI; London, 1883), I, 118.

22. *Cal. S. P., Col., East Indies, 1513–1616*, p. 357.

23. Foster (ed.), *Letters*, V, 121–23; letter dated Feb. 26, 1617.

24. *Ibid.*, p. 249.

25. William Foster (ed.), *The Embassy of Sir Thomas Roe to the Court of the Great Mogul, 1615–1619* (Hakluyt Society, 2d Ser., I; London, 1899), pp. 245–46.

26. *Ibid.*, p. iii.

27. Foster (ed.), *Letters*, V, 344.

28. *Ibid.*, VI, 111.

29. *Ibid.*, p. 143.

30. *Ibid.*, II, 265.

31. Sir George Birdwood, *Report on the Old Records of the India Office* (London, 1891), p. 56.

32. Foster (ed.), *Letters*, V, 120.

33. *Cal. S. P., Col., East Indies, 1513–1616*, p. 326.

34. *Ibid., 1617–1621*, pp. 98, 229.

35. Birdwood, *Report*, p. 46.

36. For a discussion of this controversy, see Louis B. Wright, *Middle-Class Culture in Elizabethan England* (Chapel Hill, N.C., 1935), pp. 453–55.

37. *Cal. S. P., Col., East Indies, 1513–1616*, pp. 182, 286.
38. *God be thanked* (1616), p. 30.
39. *Ibid.*, p. 22.
40. *Cal. S. P., Col., East Indies, 1617–1621*, p. 101. Because of the war, I have been unable to see any copy of Wood's book.
41. Foster (ed.), *Letters*, V, 36–38, 39–40.
42. *Cal. S. P., Col., East Indies, 1617–1621*, p. 416.
43. *Ibid.*, pp. 269, 466.

CHAPTER IV

1. Miss Susan M. Kingsbury (*The Records of the Virginia Company of London* [Washington, 1906–35], I, 98) remarks on the high purpose of the company, as declared by Sir Edwin Sandys—an ideal demonstrated by its attention "to plans for the college, by the appointment of ministers, by the collection in the churches, and by the gifts received." But Miss Kingsbury adds that "the theory that the chief motive of the enterprise was religious is not supported either by the spirit or by the data of the records."

Miss Kingsbury's Introduction gives an excellent outline of the policies of the Virginia Company and of the disputes between the Smythe and Sandys factions—a discussion outside the purpose of my study. For a more detailed consideration of the policies of the two factions and the controversies among later historians concerning the significance of the quarrel, see Wesley Frank Craven, *Dissolution of the Virginia Company* (New York, 1932), *passim*.

2. Kingsbury, I, 22.
3. *Ibid.*, pp. 31–33. See also Alexander Brown, *The Genesis of the United States* (2 vols.; London, 1890), *passim*.
4. William Symonds, *Virginia* (1609), dedication.
5. *Ibid.*, pp. 14–15.
6. *Ibid.*, p. 54.
7. Licensed in the Stationers' Register on May 8, 1609.
8. Gray, *A Good Speed to Virginia* (1609), sig. C3.

9. *Ibid.*, sig. D1.

10. Price, *Sauls Prohibition Staide* (1609), sig. F2 verso.

11. *Ibid.*, sig. F3.

12. The title-page bears the old-style date of Mar. 24, 1608. The dedication to the Bishop of London is dated May 15, 1609.

13. For a brief description of the popular interest in this expedition, see Matthew Page Andrews, *Virginia, the Old Dominion* (New York, 1937), pp. 46–47. The story of the disasters that overtook the ships is a commonplace of colonial history.

14. Crakanthorpe, *A Sermon* (1609), sigs. D2–D2 verso.

15. Benson, *A Sermon* (1609), p. 92.

16. Tynley, *Two Learned Sermons* (1609), p. 68.

17. See *A True And Sincere declaration of the purpose and ends of the Plantation begun in Virginia* (1610), p. 12.

18. Crashaw, *A Sermon . . . before . . . the Lord LaWarre* (1610), sig. D4 verso.

19. This declaration was licensed for printing on Dec. 14, 1609. Crashaw's sermon was licensed on Mar. 19, 1610. A second declaration, licensed on Nov. 8, 1610, was published immediately thereafter under the title of *A True Declaration Of The estate of the Colonie in Virginia, With a confutation of such scandalous reports as haue tended to the disgrace of so worthy an enterprise. Published by aduise and direction of the Councell of Virginia* (1610).

20. Crashaw later edited documents himself and aided in the publication of others. For example, he appears to have had a hand in the preparation of John Smith's *A Map of Virginia* (1612). The work concludes with a final note (p. 110) in which W. S. [William Strachey?], who edited the work, observes: "Captaine Smith I returne you the fruit of my labours, as Mr Croshaw requested me, which I bestowed in reading the discourses & hearing the relations of such which haue walked, & obserued the land of Virginia with you."

21. Crashaw, *A Sermon* (1610), sig. K4 verso.

22. *Ibid.*, sig. L1.

23. *Ibid.*, sigs. H1 ff.

24. See Brown, *Genesis*, I, 29–32.

178

25. J. Q. Adams (ed.), *The Dramatic Records of Sir Henry Herbert* (New Haven, 1917), p. 18.

26. Crashaw, *op. cit.*, sigs. F1 verso, G1.

27. *Ibid.*, sig. H4 verso.

28. *A True And Sincere declaration* (1610), pp. 2–4.

29. *Ibid.*, p. 25.

30. Cf. Richard Hakluyt's dedication of his translation from Ferdinando de Soto, *Virginia richly valued* (1609). See also the dedication of Pierre Erondelle's *Nova Francia: Or the Description Of That Part of New France, which is one continent with Virginia* (1609). In a long "Praemonition to the Reader," prefacing *The First Booke of the Historie of Travaile into Virginia Britannia*, prepared sometime before 1612 but left unpublished, William Strachey stresses pious motives in colonization and asserts the necessity of converting the heathen. (Hakluyt Society, 1st Ser., VI; [London, 1849], pp. 10 ff.)

31. Crashaw's dedication of Whitaker's *Good Newes* (1613), sig. A2.

32. *Ibid.*, sig. A4 verso.

33. *Ibid.*, sig. B3 verso.

34. *Ibid.*, sig. C3 verso.

35. Crashaw indicates that he had a hand in the appointment of the preachers sent to Virginia. Master Glover, a worthy minister, desiring to go to Virginia, first brought letters of recommendation to Crashaw, who interviewed him and commended him to the Council for Virginia. Crashaw notes that the Rev. Richard Buck, who had gone to Jamestown, was unknown to him until he was commended by the Bishop of London. Buck, he hints, has in hand a treatise on Virginia, which will appear shortly. If this work was ever finished, all trace has been lost. (*Ibid.*, sigs. B4 verso–C1 verso.)

36. *Ibid.*, sig. I3 verso.

37. See Craven, *op. cit.*, pp. 10–11.

38. See A. L. Maycock, *Nicholas Ferrar of Little Gidding* (London, 1938), pp. 76–77, 81.

39. Kingsbury, *op. cit.*, I, 220–21. This action took place at a

meeting of the court on May 26, 1619.

40. *Ibid.*, p. 314. At a meeting of the court, Feb. 22, 1619/20.

41. See Louis B. Wright, *The First Gentlemen of Virginia* (San Marino, Calif., 1940), pp. 97–101.

42. Copland, *Virginia's God be Thanked* (1622), p. 30.

43. *Ibid.*, pp. 9–10.

44. P. Lee Phillips, "List of Books Relating to America in the Register of the London Company of Stationers, from 1562 to 1638," in *Annual Report of the American Historical Association for the Year 1896* (Washington, 1897), I, 1251–61.

45. Kingsbury, *op. cit.*, II, 76.

46. *Cal. S. P., Domestic, James I, 1619–1623*, p. 466.

47. See Norman E. McClure (ed.), *The Letters of John Chamberlain* (Philadelphia: The American Philosophical Society, 1939), II, 67, 500, for the popularity of Donne's Paul's Cross sermons.

48. *Ibid.*, I, 284. Letter to Dudley Carleton, dated Feb. 14, 1609.

49. Sir C. Alexander Harris (ed.), *A Relation of a Voyage to Guiana. By Robert Harcourt, 1613* (The Hakluyt Society, 2d Ser., LX; London, 1926), pp. 55, 61.

50. *Ibid.*, pp. 128–29. Harcourt expressed the same pious views as are to be found in the writings of the preachers. He insisted upon the value of converting the heathen and declared that preachers of the gospel would have special favors in Guiana.

51. For an account of Lewis Hughes's career, see George Watson Cole, *Lewis Hughes, the Militant Minister of the Bermudas and His Printed Works* (Worcester, Mass.: American Antiquarian Society, 1928). This essay first appeared in the *Proceedings* of the American Antiquarian Society for Oct., 1927. A discussion of the early literature on the Bermudas is to be found in J. H. Lefroy, *Memorials of the Discovery and Early Settlement of the Bermudas or Somers Islands, 1515–1685* (London, 1877), I, *passim*.

52. Hughes, *A Letter* (1615), sigs. A3–A3 verso.

53. *Ibid.*, sig. B1.

54. Hughes, *A Plaine And True Relation* (1621), sig. A3.

55. *Ibid.*, sig. A2 verso.

CHAPTER V

1. Dedication of the fourth edition to King Charles.

2. George B. Parks, *Richard Hakluyt and the English Voyages* (New York, 1928), p. 225.

3. Susan Myra Kingsbury (ed.), *The Records of the Virginia Company of London* (Washington, 1906–35), II, 519; III, 65.

4. *Purchas his Pilgrimage* (1613), p. 634.

5. *Ibid.*, p. 625.

6. *Hakluytus Posthumus, or, Purchas His Pilgrimes*, I (Glasgow, 1905), xlii; dedication to the reader. All quotations are from this edition. For a contrast between Hakluyt and Purchas, see Parks, *op. cit.*, pp. 182, 225–29. A slight correction of this highly unfavorable picture of Purchas is to be found in Louis B. Wright, *Middle-Class Culture in Elizabethan England* (Chapel Hill, N.C., 1935), pp. 535–40. See also E. G. R. Taylor, *Late Tudor and Early Stuart Geography, 1583–1650* (London, 1934), pp. 53–66.

7. *Purchas his Pilgrimage* (4th ed., 1626), dedication to the King.

8. *Calendar of State Papers, Colonial Series, East Indies . . . 1625–1629*, p. 10.

9. *Ibid.*, p. 15.

10. *Ibid.*

11. *Pilgrimes*, XIX, 218–19.

12. *Ibid.*, pp. 222–23.

13. *Ibid.*, pp. 223–24. See also p. 231.

14. *Ibid.*, pp. 238–39.

15. *Ibid.*, p. 242.

16. *Ibid.*, pp. 252–53.

17. *Ibid.*, p. 247.

18. *Ibid.*, p. 249.

19. *Ibid.*, p. 253.

20. *Ibid.*, p. 255.

21. *Ibid.*, p. 256.

22. *Ibid.*, p. 254.

23. *Ibid.*, p. 256.

24. *Ibid.*, p. 257.

25. *Ibid.*, p. 258.

26. *Ibid.*, pp. 260–61.

27. *Ibid.*, p. 267.

28. *Ibid.*, p. 217.

29. *Ibid.*, XX, 132.

30. *Ibid.*, p. 134.

CHAPTER VI

1. For details of the various projects for settlement, see D. W. Prowse, *A History of Newfoundland from the English, Colonial, and Foreign Records* (London, 1895), pp. 51–121; and J. D. Rogers, *A Historical Geography of the British Colonies, Vol. V, Pt. IV, Newfoundland* (new ed., rev. by Sir C. Alexander Harris; Oxford, 1931), pp. 18–72.

2. Rogers, *op. cit.*, p. 56.

3. *Acts of the Privy Council of England, 1619–1621* (London, 1930), p. 419. The letter to the archbishops was dated June 30, 1621.

4. Quoted from the letter attached to the Church copy in the Huntington Library. The Hoe copy, also in the Huntington Library, has the same letter from the Bishop of London, with a note, signed by Richard Whitbourne, reading: "I pray what shall bee freely given and collected where this aboue sayd letter & booke shallbe presented to retourne the same vnto Mr. Ralph Officiall to the Archdeacon of St. Allbans to bee by him retourned as aboue sayd for mee." On the back is the endorsement, "Collected in the parish of Sandridge October the 26th 1623 two shillings. Richard Westerman vic."

5. Ed. of 1620, sigs. B1 verso–B2.

6. Ed. of 1623, sig. P4. The edition of 1620 has slightly different wording.

7. Rogers, *op. cit.* pp. 59–68.

8. Sir William Alexander, *An Encouragement To Colonies* (1624), p. 37.

9. For information about the economic depression of 1619–24, I am indebted to Professor Edwin F. Gay.

10. Richard Eburne, *A Plaine Path-Way To Plantations* (1624), sigs. B2 verso–B3.

11. *Ibid.*, sig. B3.   12. *Ibid.*, p. 96.

13. *Ibid.*, p. 97.　14. *Ibid.*, p. 70. See also p. 46.　15. *Ibid.*, pp. 91–92.

CHAPTER VII

1. James Spedding *et al.* (eds.), *The Works of Francis Bacon* (London, 1872), XIII, 21–22. The letter is dated 1616. Spedding also prints a revised version of it, made later in the same year. Bacon likewise expressed his ideas about colonies, in "Of Plantations."

2. For significant references to sermons before the King, see Norman E. McClure (ed.), *The Letters of John Chamberlain* (Philadelphia: The American Philosophical Society, 1939), II, 121, 140, 152, 299, 309, 362, 424, 451, 464, 470. See also I, 295, 453–54; II, 71, 74, 286, 289, 331, 434, 439, 443, 449, 473, 482–83, 486, 489.

3. For a more detailed discussion of this theme, see Louis B. Wright, *Middle-Class Culture in Elizabethan England*, pp. 228–96, and "The Significance of Religious Writings in the English Renaissance," *Journal of the History of Ideas*, I (1940), 59–68.

4. For a discussion of the diverse motives of colonization, see Charles M. Andrews, *The Colonial Period of American History* (New Haven, 1934–38), I, 1–21; IV, 27–77.

5. See Arthur P. Newton, *The Colonizing Activities of the English Puritans* (New Haven, 1914), pp. 13–39.

6. [Francis Higginson], *New-Englands Plantation* (1630), sig. C1 verso.

7. William Bradford, *History of Plymouth Plantation* ("Collections of the Mass. Historical Society," 4th Ser., III; 1856), p. 357.

8. Americans in California in 1846 held somewhat similar ideas about their divine appointment to occupy the earth. See Robert G. Cleland, *A History of California: The American Period* (New York, 1926), p. 193.

9. For an account of this episode, see Louis B. Wright and Mary Isabel Fry, *Puritans in the South Seas* (New York, 1936), *passim*.

10. *Ibid.*, pp. 269–321.

Index